DEIRDRE KINAHAN

Deirdre Kinahan is an award-winning playwright. She is a member of Aosdána, Ireland's elected organisation of outstanding artists. Deirdre collaborates with artists and theatres all over the world, is literary associate to Meath County Council, and has a large canon of regularly produced plays to her credit.

Her best-known plays include *The Unmanageable Sisters* (an adaptation of Michel Tremblay's *Les Belles-Soeurs*), *Rathmines Road*, *Moment*, *Halcyon Days*, *Bogboy*, *Hue & Cry*, *Melody*, *Spinning*, and her Irish Revolutionary Trilogy: *Wild Sky*, *Embargo* and *Outrage*.

Deirdre works predominantly with the Abbey Theatre, Landmark Productions and Fishamble Theatre Company in Ireland, and also collaborates with theatres in the UK (Bush, Old Vic, Pentabus, Royal Court), Europe (Stat Theatre Mainz, Ateneum Warsaw) and America (Irish Arts Centre, Solas Nua, Manhattan Theatre Club, Steep Theatre, Irish Theatre Chicago, Irish Rep NYC).

Recent works include *An Old Song, Half Forgotten* for the Abbey Theatre and SoFFt Productions, *The Saviour* for Landmark Productions, *In the Middle of the Fields* for Solas Nua, Washington DC, *The Visit* for Draiocht and Dublin Theatre Festival, and *Bloody Yesterday* for Glassmask Theatre.

Deirdre has a number of new theatre and screen projects in development. She also has years of experience as a producer, and enjoys curating or participating in multi-genre artistic projects for Meath County Council and other national festivals and events.

DEIRDRE KINAHAN: SHORTS

Five Plays

Bé Carna
Hue & Cry
Bogboy
Wild Notes
An Old Song, Half Forgotten

NICK HERN BOOKS

London

www.nickhernbooks.co.uk

A Nick Hern Book

Deirdre Kinahan: Shorts first published in Great Britain as a paperback original in 2023 by Nick Hern Books Limited, The Glasshouse, 49a Goldhawk Road, London W12 8QP

Deirdre Kinahan: Shorts copyright © 2023 Deirdre Kinahan

Deirdre Kinahan has asserted her right to be identified as the author of this work

Cover photograph: iStockphoto/andipantz

Designed and typeset by Nick Hern Books, London
Printed in Great Britain by Mimeo Ltd, Huntingdon, Cambridgeshire PE29 6XX

A CIP catalogue record for this book is available from the British Library

ISBN 978 1 84842 932 1

This book of plays is dedicated to the memory of my brilliant, brave and beautiful friend, Jo Egan.

'She is a girl would not be afraid to walk the whole world with herself' *Lady Augusta Gregory*

Contents

Introduction
Deirdre Kinahan

I am delighted by the publication of these five short plays
which feature intermittently in the swirl of my writing career
from my very first effort, *Bé Carna* (1999), to my most recent
commission, *An Old Song, Half Forgotten* (2023). They each
carry their own story as to my life in theatre, as well as reaching
out into the ether to find voice for some beautiful, broken
characters disappeared by the world.

The first play, *Bé Carna* (women of the flesh), was written in
1999 when I was working as an actress in my own fledgling
theatre company, Tall Tales. A good friend of my mother Pat,
Sister Fiona Pryle, was setting up a support group for women
working in prostitution in Dublin and asked me if I would
teach the ladies basic literacy and computer skills as a means of
subsidising my budding artistic life. I spent five years working
with this brilliant organisation, Ruhama Women's Project, now
considered to be one of the most important advocacy groups in
Ireland and Europe.

Back in the day, however, we hadn't a bob, and I remember
literally wallpapering a tiny room at the top of a shop in a
tough part of Dublin, with two of the women, to create our first
meeting place. The women accessing the project had spent most
of their lives working in prostitution. They were older now and
Ruhama was trying to help them retrain and secure a different
means of making a living, if that was their desire. Prostitution in
Dublin in the 1990s was still an outdoor/street pursuit, though
a new group of trafficked and drug-using women were growing
in number. Ruhama had an outreach service and provided a
safe space with lovely services, such as reflexology, massage,
counselling and various educational classes.

The ladies knew I was trying to make a career in theatre, so
they used to come and see me in plays produced by me and

my friend Maureen Collender through Tall Tales. Then one of
the women asked if I would write a play about them; a play
that gave a true picture of who they were as women, not just as
prostitutes. I thought it a great idea and said I would try to put a
team together, including a writer, explaining that I didn't write
for theatre. The women, however, were having none of it; they
knew me, trusted me and wanted me to write that play. So...
what to do but give it a go? And so *Bé Carna* – and Deirdre the
playwright – were born.

The play is a series of five interlinking monologues inspired by
stories I came across at Ruhama. I suppose I wanted to share
with an audience the privilege of knowledge that I enjoyed
as to how diverse and courageous this community of women
are. How they don't fit into any stereotype and how their
lives as women are deeply impacted by society's response to
prostitution. I worked with a wonderful team of five actors,
and director Gerry Morgan, in figuring out how to link and
perform these individual pieces, imagining a kind of homage
to the ghosts of Irish women subjected to institutionalisation
and vilification over the centuries. We played for a few weeks
in Dublin and took the play to Edinburgh. It was very well
received, and I believe organisations used the text for advocacy
and education around the realities of such a life for many years.
It is, understandably, a dark tale, but reverberates nonetheless
with humanity, warmth and comic humour – because that is/was
the truth of the fantastic women I knew at the time.

Hue & Cry is a very dear play to me because I believe it to be
the play where I really found my writing voice. Seven years in,
it was written as part of a programme of new plays by women
produced by Tall Tales for a lunchtime season of nine weeks.
The play is an exploration of grief and how it might shape a
human being. It was written not long after my own mother died
and was probably part of my trying to figure out how to hold
on to a happy disposition whilst facing the cruel void of her
absence. I had also experienced a miscarriage that year so was
'reeling', to quote my old pal Damian who is central to the play.

The set-up is quite traditional: it is the night before a funeral and
two cousins meet at the gathering. There is a dilemma, however,

in that the son of the man to be buried, Damian, is not welcome, and his cousin Kevin (a delicate dance choreographer) has been sent into the tiny sitting room to throw him out! The play, to me, was always like a boxing match, as these two gorgeous, broken beings shift and dance around each other before coming to a deep understanding despite themselves, and connecting in a way that one might never imagine.

Hue & Cry was originated by two great Irish actors, Will O'Connell and Karl Shiels. Karl in particular is a legendary figure, who died far too young in 2019. I was thrilled when Will took to directing a new version in the spring of that year at its original venue with two younger actors, never knowing that seeing Karl there was to be the last time I would ever encounter him.

Bogboy is my dad's favourite play, a badge that brings its own importance to my heart. My poor dad never thought I'd make a living in theatre and he spent years trying in vain to redirect me. Indeed, to this day, I'm still not sure he is entirely convinced!

The play centres around two characters, Hughie and Brigid, and their budding friendship in the bogs of Meath. This pair couldn't be less likely bedfellows, with totally different backgrounds, outlooks, accents, inner and outer lives – yet they bring great consolation to each other, as Brigid struggles with drug addiction and Hughie his mental health. They are thrown together when Brigid moves to a rural rehabilitation programme, begging lifts from her gentle, monosyllabic neighbour. As their doomed friendship grows, we get a sneak peak into their lives, but all is upended when an amnesty is announced for those involved in IRA terrorist murders during the troubled 1970s. *Bogboy* is really a play about Ireland's relationship with the Northern Irish struggle, our deep complicity in and denial of that war, told through the meeting of these two lost and lonely souls. It was originally written for RTÉ as a radio play and then adapted for the stage, winning two awards at the 2010 First Irish Festival in New York.

Wild Notes is an unusual little play, written for Solas Nua Theatre Company in Washington DC, one of many plays

written for or produced by international theatre companies as
my career moved more and more beyond Ireland. The play was
commissioned as a sister play to one written by Psalmayene
24, a hip-hop artist from Washington DC, in commemoration
of Frederick Douglass, the escaped slave and abolitionist, who
visited Ireland in the 1840s. The two plays were performed as
one production in a makeshift tent on the pier of the Anacostia
River, where Douglass once lived.

Delving into Black American history was a frightening, if
privileged, prospect, because I am a white woman with no
experience of what it is to live that often brutal reality. Frederick
Douglass, however, is a most extraordinary character, who was
greatly impacted by his trip to Ireland in 1845–46, claiming that
it was the first time in his life he was treated not as a slave but as
a man. His visit was organised by Irish Quakers who eventually
bought him his freedom, but he came at a time when the native
Irish were dying in their thousands from colonial neglect and
starvation during the Great Famine. Douglass was startled by
the plight of these white Irish, recognising the deep repression
of their race, and noting that the desperation of their music was
akin to the 'wild notes of the cotton fields' back home.

In *Wild Notes* I examine the impact of colonialism on Ireland
and America through a meeting between Douglass and a young
woman hoping to emigrate to the country he runs from, in order
to win her own freedom. Our 'Frederick Douglass Project' was
greatly celebrated in Washington in 2018 and nominated for a
suite of Helen Hayes Awards.

An Old Song, Half Forgotten was written entirely for the voice
of one of Ireland's best-loved actors, Bryan Murray. Bryan was
recently diagnosed with Alzheimer's and couldn't bear the idea
of never stepping foot on stage again, so I offered to write a play
for him that he might still perform. A crazy idea perhaps, but
then theatre is always the right place for crazy ideas.

The play is inspired by Bryan's own life but presents a different
character, James O'Brien, who is joined on stage by a charming
version of his younger self. When a string quartet visit the day
room of the older James's nursing home, the music they play

stirs a suite of fabulous moments and memories in him that take the audience on a journey through his beautifully ordinary, extraordinary life. Both James and his younger self enter into these memories in real time, re-enacting his own experiences and those of the people close to him, thus rebuilding a man just as his Alzheimer's causes him to crack and fade. It is thanks to the amazing courage of Bryan and the determined genius of my fellow creatives, under direction from Louise Lowe, that the play could reach the Abbey stage in 2023.

The short play is very traditional to Irish theatre; indeed a night of two or three one-act plays was a mainstay of early programming at the Abbey, allowing thoughts, themes and worlds to connect and collide during a single evening of theatrical entertainment. I believe it to be a little jewel of a structure, because it keeps the audience in their seats, immersed entirely in a lightning flash on a different world, the illumination made all the more acute by brevity.

The plays in this book each shine a light into a forgotten corner of our humanity, insistent in their unearthing of those disappeared by their own people – be it because of colour in *Wild Notes*, addiction in *Hue & Cry*, disease in *An Old Song*, or social boycott in *Bé Carna* and *Bogboy*. I do hope you enjoy your dance in the domain of these irrepressible characters. They have a lot to say, even if they choose to say it quickly and quietly.

February 2023

BÉ CARNA

Women of the Flesh

Author's Note

Bé Carna is written as five monologues which weave in and out of each other. I have presented the monologues in the original sequence here but it is not imperative that this sequence be followed. In the first production of *Bé Carna* directed by Gerry Morgan, the monologues are set against a compassionate female chorus comprised of the five actors. This structure grew out of workshops participated in by myself, Gerry and the five original actors: Maureen Collender, Evan Holton, Róisín Kearney, Eithne McGuinness and Victoria Monkhouse. The chorus embody the notion that these women echo the stories of all women, all times, everywhere, who have suffered because of society's inability to cope with issues around sex. The chorus represent a ghostly body who persuade these five characters to tell their stories, and in telling of their own plight in a present time frame, the characters provide for a 'remembering' of all those who have gone before. The five actors play both character and chorus member. While in the chorus they watch each character 'tell', they live each story and comfort the teller. *Bé Carna* takes place in an imaginary landscape, the gritty realism of the stories is in stark contrast to the ghostly limbo-setting of the play.

Bé Carna was first performed at Andrew's Lane Theatre, Dublin, on 5 May 1999. The cast was as follows:

GER	Eithne McGuinness
KATHLEEN	Maureen Collender
TERESA	Róisín Kearney
RACHEL	Victoria Monkhouse
SANDRA	Evan Holton
Director	Gerry Morgan
Designer	Kieran McNulty
Lighting Designer	Maeve Wright
Music	Eanna Hickey
Stage Manager	Sean Rafferty

4

Characters

GER, *forties*
SANDRA, *thirty*
TERESA, *twenties*
RACHEL, *twenties*
KATHLEEN, *forties*

*An empty stage. Five women enter. Each actor only becomes
their character when telling their story, at all other times they
form the* CHORUS. *The women form a semicircle with the actor
playing* GER, *backstage-centre. The actor playing* SANDRA
*lies down in the middle of the stage. The play opens with a
recital of the words entitled* 'Dead Sisters' *by the actor playing*
GER.

GER. Dead sisters, dead sisters, dead sisters. Grey water,
scrubbing, raw, kneeling, faceless, secrets, suck, hidden
nuns, prayers, trees, blood, heels clattering, light, dirty,
shameful-shameless-senseless-hussy, escape, your own fault
echoing, cold, dead sisters. Sunday, knuckles, whimpers,
dimples, soil, black, glass, flee, scatter, squeaks, strangle,
smother, bits-of-bones, shudder, cry, control, batter. Weeds,
backstreets, home, struggle, jagged-trousers, crotch, semen,
worried, Mother-Mary-monster-maggots, Mother-of-God,
Lucifer, burning, washing, body, desperation, isolation,
loneliness, creaking, child, loss, biting bedsheets, pain, first
time, Daddy-I'm-a-football, murder, maudlin, earth, muddy,
freefalling, fingernails, scrubbing-brush, rats, beatings,
bruises, mottled, muttering-murmur, rain, drizzle, float,
breakdown, how, hurt, dead sisters, soar, bang, friendly,
chattering, disappear, forget, fenced in, cowering, trapped,
remember, crouched, cuddling-cunt, priest, confession,
gloomy, miserable, damp-tights, hair, brushing, mammy's-
best-girl, lost, brothers, crayons, ocean, wrinkles, tears.
Dead sisters.

SANDRA *is lifted by two other members of the* CHORUS,
*who approach during the recital in a slow surreal manner.
Her hair is brushed and plaited as she is prepared to tell her
tale. The two* CHORUS *members return to their original
places and* SANDRA *begins.*

SANDRA. I had to go and meet the teacher yesterday, Miss
Clancy, Catherine. She's lovely, the arty type, great with the

kids. I didn't know what it meant when I got the letter from the school... shitting it, nearly died like I thought Daragh was in trouble or someone had complained or... I just didn't know what to think, really. It turned out it was kind of like an open day for the parents to come and see what the kids were doing in the class... (*Sigh*.)

Sure that was worse, I thought there would be loads of parents there and some of them would have their husbands and what if anyone knew me... Jesus, and what the hell would I wear? I wasn't going. But I went. And it was grand, there were only two of us mothers who turned up, pity really for the other kids. Daragh was thrilled. I was thrilled. Catherine got the kids to sing for us and then me and Marty, that's the other mother, we helped them stick tinsel and shamrocks and stuff on Paddy's Day cards. It was great. The kids are all around ya and full of business, as if a little green card was the most important thing in the world. It's a lovely warm feeling in that class, they're all so important, each kid has a part to play in the class... and there are lovely bright colours on the wall with happy faces grinnin' out at you. They're lucky kids. I can't remember any colour in school, I don't remember that buzz of work and fun. Maybe it was there but I don't hear it.

Cathy invited me and Marty back, she said she would try another open day and perhaps more mothers would come. They don't have the time in this estate, it's a pity coz when you look at the kids, I mean they are the most important, no matter what state you're in or how bad things are, they are the way out aren't they... you've got to get it together for them.

I'm determined to sort this mess out, to get it right for me and Daragh. No more men, no way, they just make trouble and debts.

I'm in so much debt.

I bought a car... was I out of my mind...? I bought a car and Jamie the bastard wrote it off. I thought if I had a car, I could bring Daragh out on weekends to parks and places, maybe

even to the zoo, away out of this kip of an estate. I read in
the library about kids' art classes in the National Gallery, I
mean wouldn't that be wonderful, imagine bringing your kid
to a place like that. I've never even been in it myself but with
Daragh I'd just be like other mothers, doing me best for him,
making an effort you know. I'd have loved that. I thought I
could maybe get a job, you know, a real job delivering stuff
maybe or anything at all, I'd be mobile, independent like.
I did eight lessons and everything, spent one hundred and
twelve pound and I was doing really great until Jamie… fuck
him, he did it out of spite, I'm convinced of it. He'd hate me
to make something of myself. You don't see prostitutes with
cars…

SANDRA *finishes and* TERESA *steps forward, they smile at
each other and* SANDRA *takes up a position in the circle.*
TERESA *begins.*

TERESA. I'm a whore, I work for an escort agency, high-class,
reliable and very discreet.

I'd like to put you straight. Most people view prostitutes as
lowlife, they have a fascination for the sexual nature of our
profession but don't like to mix with us socially. You would
like to keep us at a distance but are nevertheless compelled
to take a closer look. Even you, gentlemen, don't you get
a teeny weeny bit excited when you imagine my silk white
stockings and firm yearning tits! (*She laughs.*)

You see the media just love talking about prostitutes, makes
for great viewing figures. I've heard women on late-night
chat shows who I know don't work in the business, they are
just hired by the programme to get all the perverts to tune in.
I'm sure I would charge a large fee for the pleasure.

A girl was murdered last week so the papers are full of
comment and hooker sob stories… another rush, it's good
for business, makes the nervous type break from fantasy
and sample the goods. Apparently the girls on the streets
suffer – too many police about. To be honest I don't know
how anyone can work the streets in Dublin now, the violence

is crazy and there is no protection: drug addicts, drunks…
Jesus you'd need to be desperate to do it. I joined the agency
three years ago, best move I ever made. Clean, controlled and
payment guaranteed. My agent collects the fee and pays me
promptly in cash, any extras and I work it out with the client.
I don't even use the apartment midweek because I do the
country runs. I do enjoy the rural work, the clients tip well
and are generally far less demanding than the tourists and
Dublin men.

It's not all sex, you know. Many men just want the company,
it's important to entertain, amuse, pamper. One regular in the
north-west just likes me to bathe him, a scented scrub and a
sprinkling of baby powder. Harmless obsession. He's a gentle
man. Polite, punctual and always so silent. I often wonder
what is going on behind those weak blue eyes. I don't try to
talk, not in the job description, the last thing the client needs
is an escort blabbering on and issuing demands. You need a
good personality in this game, need to know what they need.
I tend to work straight through when I'm out of town. The
demand is enormous. Very few agencies go nationwide now,
you need to be organised and we're organised.

Jonathan has a new administrator now, dotty old tart but
efficient, she came through from the parlour, I believe. She
sets up everything on the rural run, bookings, transport, the
lot. I do so well midweek, I often take the weekend off, she'll
phone to see if I'm available and mostly I'm not. (*Pleased*.)
There are a good few girls working with 'Pleasure' now, it's
the best operation in town in my opinion. The customers are
vetted and only the most experienced and pleasing girls are
offered. No drugs. ABSOLUTELY NO DRUGS. There was
an escort, worked over six months, very popular according to
Jonathan but he found out she was taking. Fuck, he flipped,
she could have jeopardised the entire agency. The clients are
told that the girls are clean. I'll introduce her to you, Rachel
O'Neil, God, what a mess.

TERESA *returns to the circle and the actor playing*
RACHEL *moves towards* KATHLEEN *as if to avoid telling*

her tale. KATHLEEN *turns her forward towards the front of the stage and gently pushes her on.* RACHEL *goes to* SANDRA *and* GER *in the same manner; both gently push her out front.* RACHEL *is about twenty, English accent, grunge look, appearance and demeanour show signs of the chaos of her life. She begins.*

RACHEL. Little Miss fucking Professional… professional of fuck. I know her… (*Snorts in disdain.*) We worked together when I came to Dublin first, used to double up… she worked the street… but always thought she was a cut above the rest. Fuck her, fuck her agency, fuck Jonathan fuck-provider. They're all crazy, sometimes I wonder am I the only person sane. I've just come out of res, that's residential drug unit. I left, crazy place… everything is confrontation: face yourself, face the lies, face the failure, face addiction, face-fuck… I just haven't got the energy. I don't know how I let that guy Frank talk me into it, he said I could go the pace… said there were all sorts of programmes… you do some theatre, art, they even have a gym. I wanted to go in, he convinced me I needed to, but I'm not addicted. I told him, I can kick it whenever I want… They have a follow-on, you work in the country, I'd have loved that. Aisling lives in Meath, I remember loving her house, she has three dogs, they're wild. We used to walk for hours. I thought Mum must have lived in Meath, but Aisling only moved there when she got married. Her and Mum lived in Dublin. Mum never saw her house, but she says I came over when I was small. Mum couldn't cope and sent me over but then she took me back. I don't remember, I can never remember the sequence: home, not home, here, someone else's home.

That building, the res… it's so eerie, it was like a laundry or something… years ago… where women worked after they had their babies. It was a place of punishment, penance… girls went in and never came out. Imagine washing your life away behind high walls. Wishing it away I'd say. I'm sorry I heard about it. Their graves are in the grounds. I kept imagining their lives – thinking I could see them, lost there, forgotten… just because they fucked and here was I, living in the same place, when I do it for a living. What is it about sex, all those girls washing there for years and still they couldn't wash the stain away? There's a hill near Aisling's house, an old fairy hill with twisted trees growing out of the top of it. A girl haunts that hill, Eile, you can see her there at night... I've seen her... she was to be burned on that hill. Her father was a Druid priest so he had to follow the tradition... he was going to burn his own daughter for being a whore. Eile escaped, a warrior fell in love with her, and they flew... but in death she's returned, returned to that hill... Well I'm out, I just left. I left those poor ghosts to their memories and left the living ones to their face-the-world crackpot policies.

I'm out. Mum's out. I think she's dead. I should try to ask Aisling but it's so long since I left, I should never have taken that money, now I can't go back, it was a shit thing to do. (*Long sigh*.)

I'll have to get a job, well, I'll have to work. I can't stay back with Dan and Eamonn, they're in a bad way, the squat's in shit. It used to be great. We had a band, the one thing I ever wanted in my whole life and we had it, a band. We played a gig, and it was really good. Upstairs in The White Horse, we did that Bob Dylan song – 'Mozambique'. We really funked it up. Dan was brilliant on the drums, a real Afro sound. We could really have made it, I remember all our plans, the buzz. We were going to Mozambique... Mozambique, I don't even know where the fuck it is. We only played one gig. I'm sure there was meant to be more. I think I'll do it again though. Not with Dan. That's over. It can't be hard to find a band.

Róisín's gone, she's gone over four days and they haven't even moved to find her, she's been feeding both their habits for months and they never even fucking looked. That's shit. They've really lost it...

I asked down the canal and she was working Monday but no one has seen her since. She had tea in the van, the nuns remember seeing her, maybe she's gone home, maybe she'll be back.

Old crackling waltz music is heard. RACHEL *takes on the posture and demeanor of a dapper-man and gently leads the actor who plays* KATHLEEN *into a dance. She leads* KATHLEEN *to* GER *who takes up the step and passes her on to* SANDRA, *who in turn twirls her to* TERESA. KATHLEEN *is left twirling alone in the circle in reverie, she stops and comes forward. She is a thin, nervous type, in her forties.*

KATHLEEN. I wasn't always in this business you know. Oh, when Richard and Caroline were children I'd never have had the time. You know what children are like… everything has to be dropped. Their lives take priority… Mom's taxi, that's what I called the car! (*Cigarette.*) Of course they're the busy pair now, Richard runs an IT business in London and Caroline is in the fashion industry, she specialises in home-spun fabrics, new Irish designs… she has a boutique on Long Island. I have trouble keeping up with the pair of them.

Caroline was marvellous when her father died, I don't know how I'd have got through it without her… the telephone never stopped, 'Mom do you need anything, can I send some cash, Sean and I never stop thinking about you.' Herself and Richard sent beautiful wreaths to the funeral – freesia from a loving daughter and lilies from a broken son. Caroline even put a poem on hers:

'My loving dad,
I am so sad to see you gone,
Enjoy the light of heaven's night,
And God's loving son.'

She was always very talented. Maureen, of course, wouldn't put the wreaths on the coffin. 'Stop that nonsense,' she snaps. 'Will you not have a bit of respect at your own husband's funeral?' (*Falls quiet.*)

Sean is the latest on the mat… I wonder will she ever settle down, Caroline, and have a family. She is always joking about what a worrier I am, that's it… once a mother always a mother. (*Confiding.*) I think I'm a bit of a mother-figure to some of the girls in here, to be honest. The office is situated

in the same building as the parlour. First thing every morning
I put the phones on hold and make the girls a nice cuppa.

You're the important ladies, I say, without you there wouldn't
be a business. Kind of like a catchphrase greeting, they
seem to enjoy it. There seems to be a renewed interest in the
agency, various journalists are often on the phone. The other
morning a gang of them just burst in the door, said they were
looking for Jonathan. Well I sent them packing; microphones,
gadgets, cameras. As if I haven't enough to do. One cheeky
devil took a photograph just as he came in the door. We offer
a confidential service, I don't give out information. There
is someone here around the clock, amazing the amount
of clientele, all sorts... (*Knowing look.*) Jonathan vets the
customers, we are an exclusive organisation you know...
The office now could do with a lick of paint, I've said it to
Jonathan – 'doesn't create the right impression when you
enter the premises' – he agrees, offered to pay for the paint
if I'd have a go. Well I laughed... 'Leonardo Walker', I told
him, that's what the children called me! A nice lemon maybe
or duck-egg blue. (*She surveys the premises.*) It would have
been nice to have it done before the cameras arrived.

KATHLEEN *finishes and returns to her original place in the
circle. The chorus now start to speak,* SANDRA *first and
then the others overlapping. They walk through the circle and
about the stage,* GER *walking all the time from backstage-
centre to front – this is the preparation for her story. They
speak the following words:*

SANDRA/CHORUS. Fifteen pound for a handjob; Frightened
   the shite outta me: Car; Lonely face; Lurking; Look up and
   down; Check lock; Check out; Cold; Check corner; Inane
   fucking questions; Fifteen pound for a handjob...

TERESA/CHORUS. Run to the corner; Bitch; I forgot to go to
   Dunnes; Stand; All right; Shoes; Hurry up; Big fuckin' deal;
   Funny; Isolated...

KATHLEEN/CHORUS. Walk; Wasting; Nurture; Run to bed;
   Fuckin freezin'; Stupid cow; What do you want for dinner?;
   Lonely; Bastard...

RACHEL/CHORUS. What's in the bushes?; Lookin' for business? How much? I'm a mother you know; Ma; Waste of time; Looking; Waiting and waiting; Wasted...

As GER *moves forward she repeats the odd phrase from each character. At a signal they all stop and* GER *begins:*

GER. She's just sitting there out on the green, Amanda Dunne... sitting there waiting to die. Just a kid. Dead already. I went out to her yesterday, offered her an orange, probably a stupid thing to do but she's tormenting me, she's like a ghost out there... waiting, there's not a spark of life in her eyes. Wasted she is. You don't expect to watch kids die, it's not in the right order or something. Drugs have swept through here like a plague, that's the truth of it, like a plague from Bible times. Thank God my two young ones haven't touched them, I'd crucify them. I mean my Katie palled round with Amanda Dunne, she was a lovely kid... I can remember her running through here, shorts and sandals... it's desperate to look at her now. There does be a gang of them out on the green, all the same... wasted, hunted-looking, crazed they are from it. No one lets their kids out to play there now, you have to keep them in. I think mine are through it now, two more years in school and they'll be getting jobs, lives of their own. It's not been easy keeping them straight, I'm not saying there's not lovely kids round here, lovely families but so much despair... People are hurt here, angry and hurt, when there's no work, you get despair. Sure Grainne can't get her young fella to go back to school, fourteen and he just won't go. I mean what do ya do with him, he hasn't a chance if he's no school, ripe for the drugs. She's worried sick but what can she do, the auld fella doesn't give a shit, he's so low himself he thinks it's all a waste of time. Mike never got over that redundancy, the bastards never even paid his stamps. He got nothing after twenty years of work. Ohh, it'd drag you down if you let it. I was on the edge meself early on, SUPER-CUNT had left, two small kids and I only twenty-one. Nineteen, I was, having Kate. Thought I'd never have a baby, get a house of me own... it was just an escape, away from the madness of me ma's. Well I couldn't have picked a greater CUNT than

Brian Malone, fucking useless. He beat me so bad one night, I jumped through the bedroom window, sat there in the grass with me ankle snapped and he flings open the hall door to have another bout… straight for me face, he loved to crack me face, boot going and I trying to reef meself up – vomiting from the pain in me leg… only for Grainne and Mike I'd have been killed, he was mad, he wouldn't have stopped. (*Pause*.) Jesus, what brought me there, I haven't thought about that for years, it must be looking at Amanda, it'd get you down. That CUNT is so long gone Kate and Sinead don't even ask about him, he's officially a forgotten CUNT… almost.

GER *takes up a position in the circle, the next round of monologues are delivered with characters standing stock-still and at a rapid-fire pace.*

RACHEL. Everything is shit. My head's in shit. I'm off the drugs, I know I can do it but it's hard. I still do a little E to get high but no heroin. I'm okay but there's still no Róisín, I don't know where to look. I've lived with her eight months and I don't even know where she's from, I never thought of that before, I suppose I never asked.

SANDRA. Sharon called around yesterday. Her and Dave have had a bust-up. Really bad like. Her face is in bits. I told her she should go to the hospital but it's like talking to a brick wall. I hate Dave. I've always hated him. He used to hang around with me brother Mat. He was always leering, taking the piss, he just gives me the creeps. He used to torment me at work. 'How's business San, don't you look good tonight?' I don't know how Sharon sticks him, he's always chatting up other girls. She thinks I'm amazing the way I told Jamie to go. I suppose it's different when you have a kid, you've got to think of more than just yourself. And then again Jamie's not bad, he's not violent like. Dave is always beatin' her. I wouldn't let him inside my house.

GER. I'm cleaning the library now, been cleaning the centre for the past two years, now the library is included. It's not a bad job, started when Grainne asked me to cover for her,

I'd never have had the nerve to go looking for it meself. Anyway I was delighted when it came up, I've never looked back, three pound fifty an hour and it doesn't interfere with me welfare. I clean the offices, the crèche, the library, toilets and reception. I start at five. The offices and crèche do be empty but the library is open late-night Thursday. It's a great facility, there is a room off it where the kids do drama classes and art after school. The little ones, I love looking in at them. Your woman has a CD player and when the music stops they have to freeze like statues. Gas, they love that one, and she has another one with balls, where they throw the ball and call out their name or something, seems great fun for them. I was thinking I'd use it for me course, I'm doing a childcare course with the Fas. Qualifies you to work in a crèche, minding the kids. I heard about it through a scheme in town, they helped me register and that. I've to do a project and everything, but it's early days. I'm enjoying it. There's no pressure in this job, I'm me own boss, so long as everything is attended to every evening, no one asks any questions.

TERESA. That phone just hasn't stopped. I leave the machine on or just disconnect. Jonathan came around last night and started throwing his weight around… Where the hell am I? There are clients getting mad, I owe him money, he can't run a business with unreliable girls… he looked broody… broke two cups.

KATHLEEN. Mr Kane and I had lunch earlier, in Café Rouge, if you wouldn't mind. He is a very interesting man, mad into the computers, loves to baffle me with ROM memory, modem and the like. Talks non-stop about email and spreadshoot facilities, fascinating really. That's twice now we've had lunch. He calls me on the mobile, knows I work nearby. He likes to eat with his fingers, Mr Kane.

RACHEL *now takes up her story at normal pace.*

RACHEL. I went out to work last night and this bloke pulled up for business. I got in and I felt something kicking at my back, I looked around and this bloke's toddler is in the back of the car. I fucking flipped… just a little kid, all strapped in…

smiling, like. Sick bastard... he was going to screw me with his little kid in the back seat. I got out of the car... told him he was sick.

I did all right, I'm trying to put some cash away, to get out of the squat.

I bought a card... for Aisling... Happy Birthday Dear Aunt... don't even know if it's her birthday but fuck it, I thought it was nice. I have it in my coat. I'll ask if maybe I could visit, I need somewhere to chill out. Aisling's all right, she knows I had it tough with Mum, she's the forgiving type. She was there for one of the attempted suicides... can't remember which one... but it wasn't long after that she brought me away, back to Meath. Mum went mad, kept phoning and crying down the phone. Asking me to sing her a song. Aisling wouldn't let me back to England... she said it wasn't safe, Mum was too far gone.

I used to find my mum with razors... ketchupped in blood... I was only around nine the first time. We'd been to the DHSS for something, we used to go sometimes to get a place to stay. Mum would send me to the counter to cry. Well I couldn't cry that day. I didn't want to, so I sang. I'd learnt this song in school and loved it. (*Sings 'What a Wonderful World'.*) Fuck did that have some effect, there wasn't a dry eye in the house. My pockets were bursting with coins. I'd sing that song at the drop of a hat after, but it never met with the same success. It made Mum laugh... she hardly ever laughed.

I hadn't been to school for a year when Aisling came, I'd been fostered at least once but then Mum had got me back. She was straight for a while but then it started again... she used to bring blokes home... she was always strung out, sometimes hysterical and then the razor would come out. Fuck, I can't let it get that bad, if I could just get out, get away for a bit. I'll ask Aisling, maybe Róisín could come.

SANDRA. I used to call around a lot. To Sharon. We'd have a few drinks. I suppose we used to get a bit pissed. Well it was hard early on. Having Daragh, there was no da and me

ma didn't want to know. I'd bring Daragh around like, I'd
never leave him on his own. We'd have a laugh, me and
Sharon, Daragh was grand, she adores him... we'd just have
a few gins. I stopped calling when I met Jamie. He thought
Sharon was bad news, thought I shouldn't be drinking having
Daragh and that. I suppose he was right really. I hate it now,
getting pissed, but I missed Sharon, she was me pal. Too
good for that shit, Dave. I remember sitting in the local once,
I was with Sharon and a whole gang. Dave was out of his
face. He kept talking about the old days, him and me brother
Mat, all the craic. He kept grinning over at me. A big fucking
wide-arsed grin. I couldn't relax, I just knew he was going
to start. He loves tormentin', Dave. Loves to see you squirm.
'Little Sandra Doyle,' he was saying, 'wild woman weren't
ya when you were a kid.' Everyone was laughin'... Good old
Dave, Gas Man – him and Matt Doyle, crazy pair. I told him
to shut fuckin' up but he wouldn't stop. 'We're old friends,
aren't we San, sure you're the best little ride I ever had and
you only twelve.' He roared laughin'... everyone laughed...
even Sharon... like he hadn't said it... or it didn't matter...
pretendin' it was all a bit of fun... well I didn't laugh. Stupid-
cunt-of-a-bastard, he might have had a go when I was a kid
but I'm me own person now. I'm a mother. He had no right to
say that. No right. Who the hell is he anyway... ooh the big
man. Takes a big man to beat up his girlfriend, all right, or
cod a clueless kid.

Poor Sharon, she should give him the boot. She'd a present
for Daragh when she called. He isn't five till May, she knows
that, I thinks she just wanted to talk. She brought a bottle
but I wouldn't take a drop. I'd to collect Daragh. I wanted
her to go really but she was so upset. I let her stay. Daragh
was delighted to see her, it was her first time around since
Jamie'd left. She dotes on Daragh, she loves kids. She never
had one with Dave, he wasn't interested, has two of his own
with his wife thanks very much. Wanker. He's ruined her life.

KATHLEEN. I wonder will Mr Kane be at the set-dancing
on Thursday, that's where we met. He said he might not
make the class due to prior commitments. I wonder where

he lives... He works at the Department of the Marine, Blackrock, perhaps, or Dun Laoghaire. I can see him tending a rose garden to the soothing whoosh of the sea... his mariner's cap thrown hastily on the teak garden bench. Very light on his feet, as they say, familiar with all the sets... fluent Irish speaker as well. Country, I'd say, there's a definite lilt in his voice, especially when he gets fired up about internetting super-highways and the like.

He suggested we meet for a drink at the weekend.

The dancing classes are a lot more conducive to socialising than the single scene, it's a bit public on reflection. Still that's where I met Jonathan, Sach's Singles, and, as I said to Caroline, there had to be some way of meeting people after her father died. 'You can't stay moping behind four walls,' she said, 'you need to get out, Mum.' And out I got. Jonathan gave me the job in the parlour and dear God did that need organising, a shambles when I arrived... no filing system, ad hoc diary... Jonathan's sister took the calls and she's no head for the business, she works well as an escort I'll admit, but they needed someone with experience to put a system together. 'I worked four years as a secretary before marrying Michael,' I said to Caroline, 'all those skills sat dormant but were not forgotten.' She's very supportive. Says she knows Mum will make a success.

TERESA. I have to work today, have got to go back. Jonathan can't understand my tiredness, it's like a drug, I can never get up, can't leave the bed. My legs are dead weight and my head is cotton wool. I've taken my tablets but no effect. I woke up and it's dark because I've missed the daylight. I'll just have to get up, eat and go to work.

(*Pause, as she hits the real issue.*)

Daddy's sick. My mother phoned and said 'Daddy's sick.' Something to do with his heart and do I want to come home. I can't... I can't pretend. 'Hannah's here,' she said. I hope the bastard dies, I said... but it didn't come out, just 'Oh.' Daddy was my first client, he gave me money for clothes and

stuff, money for being his special girl... I can't remember
how it started, there was a time when he was a super dad. He
took us to the pantomime at Christmas and swimming on a
Saturday morning. He used to watch us from the side seats
and wave when we'd reach the end of the pool. The proud
dad, people always said how he loved his two girls. It was
happening for years, I never said it to Hannah, never said it
to Mam. He'd collect me from school trips and bring me up
the mountains, he never left me alone. I thought everyone
knew, could feel it in their stare... she's the girl who does
things with her da. I couldn't stop him, I couldn't tell them
and I couldn't leave... I just went to bed, Mam would be
up thinking I was sick and I'd say anything just to not have
to go into school. I couldn't face them, I thought everyone
knew. Then he'd come in and Mam would ask him to see
how I was... he'd be full of sympathy, genuinely concerned.
I thought if I was sick he'd stop, so I'd stay in the bed...
but he'd come in, Mam would be shopping on a Saturday
morning and he'd come in... he'd lift up the covers and start
feeling... and I couldn't stop him... and I'd hear Hannah
watching the cartoons and I'd be terrified she'd find us and
tell Mam. I don't think I ever even told him to stop, maybe I
did... he never heard.

I used to leave, in a strange way I'd just leave him and my
body and head off in a dream. I'd kind of shut off the action
and fall into my mind. There I could do wonderful things...
fly, like Peter Pan, or swim under the sea. I had heard an old
story about a boy who had wings made from the feathers of
a thousand birds. He could fly around the world but one day
he flew too close to the sun and the wax in the wings melted
so he fell to the earth. I was careful never to go too close,
I could just circle its golden world, then swoop down to a
beach in the Caribbean before sailing off again through the
clouds. If I flew too close to the sun I'd be forced to go back,
not when I was alone but while Daddy was still there... I had
to be careful, even in my dream not to get too close. Daddy
was like a giant shadow over my life... always looming...
always there. It started getting crazy. Even with Mam in

the house he'd start, always talking low, forcing me to do
it, laughing when I said I'd tell. 'Sure who would you tell,
Teresa, wouldn't they think you were an awful slut, messing
around with your own da.' He was right. I was trapped. Then
I think he began to get nervous. As I got older he started
patrolling the garden when I'd be out with my friends...
constantly interrogating me about boys. Always on about
my clothes... wasn't I the right little tart. The bastard was
obsessed. One night when I came home, he started tearing
at me, belting me and mauling me at the same time. 'Where
were you till this hour, little bitch...' He kept roaring about
having reared a right whore, I flipped... I spat I spat and
yelled and kicked and screamed and tore... screamed for all
those years, kicked for all those years. (*Stops*.) I don't know
what happened then... I remember hearing Mam. He must
have knocked me out, I woke up in the hospital, broken jaw,
Mam was crying 'What happened Teresa, what's wrong
with you love?' and I couldn't tell, she's so gentle, I couldn't
tell... I could just. Never. Tell.

I had to go home, but he now stayed well clear. 'That'll keep
you quiet,' he said, about the wiring in my jaw. I just took to
the bed. Eventually I left home. Drifted. School was a lost
cause, I'd missed so much over the years. I got work in a bar
in town, a bouncer told me I could earn a lot of money... and
well, here I am.

The tables are turned now, I choose who I fuck with. I say
yes or no. I see that hungry look and I decide, I put a price
on it and I take control. I no longer have to fear the sun, I can
stay where I am, I can BE ME.

GER. I can't resist flickin' through the books, when I'm doing
the library. I've joined and all now, have a few books going
the whole time. I was never into readin', but now with the
kids looking after themselves and the nights down to the
very odd one, I enjoy sitting down to a good book. I heard a
fella saying, 'When you like to read, there is never enough
time in the day.' I thought that was good. I was in there last
Thursday, fixing a few books and this auld one comes over

asking me about books for dying at home. She must have thought I worked there, not cleaning like but with the books. There was no one else around so I took her to the section, they've a great selection you know *Dying with Dignity*, *Death of a Loved One*, *Last Moments in the Home*, so I was showing her around all sensitive, like, 'Yeah that's lovely love,' she says, 'but I was thinking more of fabrics, dyeing fabrics at home.' I nearly died, I was so scarlet I couldn't even speak. She didn't seem to mind, mindya. Jesus (*She smiles.*)

GER *laughs gently and is joined by the other members of the* CHORUS, *the laugh builds and they move around the stage, throwing phrases from their stories at each other. They laugh more and more hysterically until eventually hushed by* SANDRA, *who wants to get on with her tale.*

SANDRA. I met Jamie last night. I gave him eight hundred pounds off the car.

The CHORUS *laugh.*

I don't know how it works, no matter how much I pay I still seem to owe a small fortune. I should never have let Jamie organise it with Mooney, sure he owes him a fortune himself from his different scams.

He was angling to come back. Says he misses me and Daragh. He was all gentle with the big sad eyes.

Small laugh again from the CHORUS.

He's really not the worst you know. Big dreams, like a kid. One week he's buying a boat to start fishing an' the next it's a video store. He was seriously thinking of starting up a balloon company. Hot-air balloons, that you sit in, like. Hot air is right! He even had a jingle: 'Beat that traffic sigh, go on just balloon by.'

The CHORUS *erupts with laughter.*

...fucksake, he was laughed out of the pub on that one.

Laughter now goes as they concentrate on the story.

I was almost tempted last night… it gets lonely… but no I said forget it. I'm determined to pay off this car, get Daragh into first class and then get a job. A proper job. They're always advertising courses in the community centre and the library. I just don't need Jamie's complications. I'm keepin' the head down for a few years and I'll get sorted… I don't want to be workin' the streets as Daragh gets older.

Lights down, one up only on RACHEL.

RACHEL. There was an attack last night, one of the women was badly done.

She was working down the lane, the cunt waited till he was finished then he grabbed her by the throat.

The CHORUS *start to chant beneath* RACHEL'*s firing voice.*

CHORUS. A blade apart, tear her heart, dig your fist, snap her wrist, clench and twist, a blade apart, tear her heart, dig your fist, snap her wrist, clench and twist, slap and maim, she's on the game. (*If possible these two lines are delivered when* RACHEL *says 'Stanley'.*)

RACHEL. 'Give us your cash you little slut.' She was only out but she gave him what she had… she thought he turned to go but then she saw the flash of steel… he fucking sliced her face up with a Stanley.

Light up on SANDRA.

SANDRA *continues*.

SANDRA. I must have crawled down the lane, I don't remember anything but I must have reached the road because a taxi driver found me and took me to hospital. They've had to stitch back my nose. (*She sobs.*) I was only out, I should never have chanced him, I suppose he looked kind of rough. The nurse says they'll do their best but it's likely there'll be scars… What did I do, I gave him the money and everything. (*Cries inconsolably.*)

TERESA. Jonathan is starting to bug me. Prowling round the flat – issuing demands, looking for more time. It's time to move on… I'm not going to suffer him. 'There's plenty a

pretty face down the line.' (*Shrugs*.) As if I can't see them
coming. Well I've got my regulars, I can go out on my own.
I know how it works, it's not so difficult to set up or I could
always change tack... there's a bunch of nuns offering
courses... now I don't know what their game is, probably out
to save some souls. The Legion were at it for years, offering
tea and praying, waste of time.

This crew do computers: training, stuff like that... their entry
system's terrific... so long as you fuck for a living you're in.
It'd be useful though, no matter what I decide... I mean at
the moment everything's fine but I don't intend to be on my
back for the rest of my life. I've never done anything else bar
that brief stint as a barmaid... I'd call if I knew the set-up,
they could start hassling me, some of these do-gooders just
don't give you a break. Prostitution can be like a magnet for
those who want someone to save.

RACHEL. Róisín's dead. I heard this morning. She was found
in a flat. Dead. Stabbed to death. Stabbed. She's from Bray,
beside the sea. She never mentioned that.

Her parents are in the papers, appealing for information. I
went to the squat to get her stuff for them but there's nothing
left. I asked Dan and Eamonn but they're so fucked... there's
nothing left.

KATHLEEN. Maureen was on this morning. Crisis gathering.
The Sunday papers are doing an investigation into the
thriving sex business in Ireland. 'Vice Queen Awaits Morning
Appointment', and a picture of me sitting behind my desk.
I haven't seen it, won't look. It's there on the coffee table
where Maureen flung it. Amazing how harmless it looks,
folded and inert.

I've always hated these family conflabs as she calls them,
I've always been at the centre and I can never seem to find
a voice. Dear God she was really rattling this morning,
hysterical I'd call it, quite an amazing amount of fuss.

Harry and Chris, the hubbies, came also, sat in their
Crombies looking miffed. My sister Denise insisted we shut

the curtains, she tripped twice coming up the drive with a chiffon scarf draped over her head. The two of them, sat like vipers, ready to do battle, wielding their family success. The Dalkey Demons, Caroline calls them, she'd soon put them in their place.

It appears there was an argument as to where the conflab should take place but seeing as neither would have me set foot in their house, this was the only venue. Needless to say I wasn't consulted.

The two of them sitting there whispering, exactly as they've done all my life. I could sense the same glee as D-Day in St Mary's School when I went to enrol Richard for class. Michael had thought my fantasies harmless until I started to talk to outsiders about them and of course Maureen always ready to stick her nose in, couldn't let anything rest. (*Rising, upset, starting to blow.*) Whisper, whisper to the principal, when I'm standing there with the enrolment form. 'Harry's out in the car Kathleen, hop out now and we'll give you a lift home.' I didn't get a chance to speak. Whisper, whisper followed by sympathetic smiles from Father Kirwin. 'Harry's in the car Kathleen – (*As Maureen, whispering.*) sorry about this, Father, she's never been quite right. (*Up a pitch.*) Come along Kathleen now stop this nonsense at once, Father Kirwin is a busy man we mustn't waste his time with a child who doesn't exist.' (*STOP for a second.*)

(*Angry, fast.*) Ooh she revelled in saying that. As if I didn't know Richard was a lie. She had to rub my nose in it. Michael must have phoned her to get me to stop, the two of them: whisper, whisper, whisper, it never stopped. 'There is no Richard, Kathleen you know that and Caroline's a fiction dear, stop this ludicrous behaviour, go home to your husband and sort yourself out.' 'Sort yourself out', as if it were that simple. Slip back into oblivion Kathleen, watch Michael walk out into life and sit admiring your maple floorboards. She has no idea, no conception of life without event. I sat for years in that lonely house with big bay windows built for children to look out at raindrops. Everyone had babies, but it never happened for me, not once. No morning sickness or swollen breasts. God, I wanted it so much. Years of yearning but I just dried up. Michael said to be patient but how could I when all around were cradling and children laughing in the street. Well once I did think I was pregnant, the monthlies were late. So I bought a pair of little pink booties... so sweet, little lacy fronts. Later I saw a matching baby coat, well I knew I wasn't pregnant but I thought 'just in case'. I suppose it became a bit of a habit after that. Little shoes... teddies and dolls. First I had Caroline, I mean I knew it wasn't real but it gave me a purpose, something to talk about at the shops. Then two years to the day, Richard arrived. Perfect, a girl and a boy like I'd always wanted. Michael never interfered. But Maureen, she always liked to ruin things. That day, after the incident at the school, she raided Richard's room. Took everything, she said I had to 'cop myself on'. She took everything, his new school shoes, even his aeroplane collection. Well I let her think she'd won, I never mentioned them in public after that.

GER. I'm doing a book for kids, it's part of the course. You do it in sections; hygiene, play, physical development and psychology. As part of the play end I have to write a short story for children and illustrate it. I didn't know where to start, panicked I was. But Kate says, 'Ma, do you remember the magic shoe stories you used to tell us, use one of them.' And do you know, she was dead right. I had reams of them. Magic yellow shoes with pink heels and bows which when you wore them took you to far-off magic lands. We used to dance our way through bedtimes, we did. So here am I at my age with scissors and glitter and paint and crayons and the whole lot, like something out of *Blue* bleedin' *Peter*. Some of the others in the class are doing it on computer, brilliant pictures and everything... that made me a bit nervous but Sorcha, that's me tutor, said mine looked very imaginative and colourful (*Gives an unconvinced look*.) Well I suppose I'm not bad at drawin' and I used all different materials in the pictures, coz kids love feelin' things. I've nearly finished it. A little girl travels to Alaska in the shoes and meets Santa

frozen in the ice, she sets him free and brings him back to
Lapland with the shoes. I was afraid it was crap but the kids
said it was good.

I'm starting the placement soon. You can't get on this course
without a placement. Most of them are already working in
crèches, so they have a head start but sure I reared two of
me own. I start in the crèche here in two weeks. Some of the
office workers have their kids in it and local mothers can use
it when they're havin' counsellin' or using the library. Fiona
runs it. She's grand, says she's looking forward to the extra
pair of hands. I'm just in two mornings to start with... see
how I get on. I'll keep up the cleaning but you never know,
apparently there's a huge demand for trained carers. Sorcha
reckons I'll be great, having had a family and that. Jesus
won't it be great. A new world, I mean I never paid any heed
in school, just knocked around looking for a bloke to take
me away from the auld fella and the auld one. Do you know
you can waste your whole life, can't ya. Throw it away when
you're in your teens, when you don't know your arse from
your elbow. It's rare you get the second chance. I mean take
Amanda Dunne and what about that young one who was
murdered, Jesus it's desperate... She went back to a flat from
the canal... stabbed over twenty times according to Jackie.
Slashed apart. There are so many young ones out now, Jackie
says there's a new face every night and you just can't talk to
them. It's the drugs, cost a fortune, three hundred pound a
day one kid said. The risks they take. Crazy. I rarely go out
at all now. I'd give it up altogether if I had the money. The
square isn't as bad as the canal but Jackie reckons it'll soon
be overrun. Bloody war, there'll be. There used to be a code,
well at least we all looked out for each other, but sure now
you wouldn't know half of them. I don't like going out, I'm
getting on and I can't stand the cold. Some nights I go home
with less than I had going out, there's always a new face. I'll
be glad to get out, it can drain the lifeblood out of ya. Last
week I had a young fella, eighteen if he was a day. Started
bawlin' his eyes out doin' the business, I gave his head a little
rub and, not thinking, I kissed him. He spat in my face.

My whole life I've been looking over my shoulder, frantic
someone would find out and tell the kids. (*Cringes*.) Jesus
I still can't think of it, can't face the thought. And there's
always people around; journalists, researchers, religious,
gawkers, goody-goody do-gooders, lunatics that would drive
you mad. I only ever wanted to work and go home. Some of
the girls got involved, you know with feminists and that. Not
me, it was bad enough with the kids and joyriders gawkin'
without that other shower. One time there was a march, years
ago, all these auld ones roaring about women reclaiming
the night – bloody marvellous – not a punter could get
near the place, that was the one thing we had – the bloody
night. Some of the women got involved in the health centre,
educating the nurses. They'd give interviews to the press and
all! Jesus, not me, I'd rip a camera apart if someone took
a photo. There was one of Jackie once, they coloured out
the head but if you knew her you knew who it was. Fuck.
(*Shakes head*.) I wonder will she ever give it up. Tommy
still drives her down and picks her up. Tommy Turf, always
betting on the horses and never worked a day in his life.
Jackie might as well work direct for Paddy Power. I suppose
she's happy enough. She never says.

Well when I have my course, there'll be no stopping me. It'll
be a whole new different life.

SANDRA. Jamie came to visit again today. He's taking Daragh
back home. Sharon was mindin' him. I hope that bastard
Dave's not been near him… I told Jamie I want him home.
I'll get out of here soon, I have to see him. He's not been in
coz Jamie thought I was too upset. He says he'll bring him in
to me this evening. Poor little mite, two whole days without
his ma. Jamie told him I was sick… I hope he doesn't cry
when he sees the state of me. I can barely look at meself.

The scar starts here – (*Points to right cheek*.) and goes right
across my nose to here. (*Left cheek*.) It's red and raw and I
won't go outside the door unless I have to. I can't stand the
sight of it, Jamie says it soon will fade but I don't think so.
It screams at me from the mirror. I have nightmares about

that knife. It walks all by itself stalking me and Daragh.
Jamie's been looking for the bloke who did it. Him and Mick
Mooney are going to tear him apart. He put the word out and
one of the girls reckoned she knew who did it.

He's been brilliant, Jamie... the best. He even lets Sharon
come round again. We have a few jars at home... I need to let
off steam. I'm too nervous to go out yet. And Daragh loves
Sharon, he loves Jamie too. I suppose he needs a dad... he
really loves having him around and I don't know where I'd
be for the shoppin' and that.

Daragh's teacher phoned, Cathy. She's havin' another one
of those open days... thought I might like to help organise
it. I was a bit worried, with me face still raw like, and Jamie
says you're better off keepin' your distance... I suppose he's
right... I'll wait till things get straightened out... sure we can
start again, then... we can start again tomorrow.

SANDRA *finishes, unravels her hair and moves back into
the circle, her story is told.*

KATHLEEN. The parlour will no doubt close down. I've not
heard a word. The Dalkey Demons have severed all relations.
Not that that will make much difference, I never saw them.
Maureen says I can't shame them any more, I'm a filthy
disgusting harlot, apparently, unfit to be their sister. Denise
says the neighbours will want me to move, I'm a bad element
in the area. I said, 'I don't speak to my neighbours, they
don't know me,' but it didn't seem to matter.

Funny there's been no word from Mr Kane.

KATHLEEN *looks around at each of the women and moves
back into original position. Her story is told.*

RACHEL. I phoned Aisling. I intended to be cool but something
snapped... I told her about Róisín and the squat and the res
and the drugs... Déjà vu... she must have thought she was
listening to Mum. I fucked up, I know. Aisling brought me
back and gave me a home, sisters, dogs. I couldn't sit still,
couldn't see it. I had to fuck it all up. Got thrown out of

the school, fucked about with the lads from town. I wanted
to show I was a city girl... I wanted them to see that I was
different... cool, experienced, fun... I think I wanted it to be
fucked coz that's how it always had been. Aisling took it all.
Three years I fucked with her family and then I left. Robbed
her cash and left.

She says I can come down. Never mentioned the money.
Wondered for years where I went. She said she crawled
the town for days after I'd gone, contacted the guards in
Dublin, nationwide. Jesus, they've arrested me often enough,
amazing they never twigged. Everyone thought I'd gone back
to England she said.

Says I can come if I agree to visit a centre in Navan. Says
she'll help me start again. She sounds so like Mum... I'm
getting the bus tomorrow. (*She says this in a way that means
you don't know whether she actually will.*)

RACHEL *also looks around, takes original position, her
story is told.*

TERESA. I phoned the God Squad. Well first three digits... it
got me out of bed. Sometimes I feel I've spent my whole life
in bed... bed to escape the fuck, bed to take the fuck. One
morning I'd like to get up and not fuck.

She looks to GER, *the last remaining character, and takes up
her original position, her story is told.*

GER. I can't get used to not having a class. Keep thinking I
should be studying or something. I had me final essay and
all started. I was going to do it on drama for children. I'd
talked to your woman who ran the class in the library. She
arrived in with a load of books this evening. I never said
anything. Amn't I the eejit telling the world about it. Me and
my course. Fool, fool, fool, fool, fucking fool. What was I
thinking...

(*Looks to audience.*) You need a police check to work with
kids. It's standard practice apparently. What the fuck could I
do, say? I was done a few times for soliciting, years back...

but still. I'm not having that dug up. Had to leave the course. I let on the placement fell through, then Sorcha wanted to organise something else... shit! So I said I wanted to spend more time with the kids. She wasn't convinced. I knew by her. Well I could hardly tell her I was a whore. WAS wouldn't matter. WAS is AM.

Each member of the chorus repeats this to fade...

GER. WAS IS AM...

SANDRA. AM IS WAS...

KATHLEEN. WAS AM IS...

RUTH. IS WAS AM...

TERESA. AM WAS IS...

The End.

HUE & CRY

Hue & Cry was first performed at Bewley's Café Theatre, Dublin, on 20 June 2007. The cast was as follows:

DAMIAN   Karl Shiels
KEVIN   Will O'Connell

Director   David Horan
Costumes   Jo Richards
Costume Assistant   Aoife Davis
Sound Designer   Marian McEvoy
Choreographer   Kieran McNulty
Production Manager   Eileen Sheridan
Stage Manager   Jo Richards
Production Assistant   Sara Cregan
Designer   Steve Neale
PR/Marketing Manager   Conleth Teevan

Characters

KEVIN
DAMIAN

We are in the small front room of a South Dublin council house. It is set up for a funeral. There are candles, flowers, bottles of alcohol and mounds of sandwiches on a small table. We never move outside this room and there is no break in the dramatic action.

It is late in the evening. DAMIAN *stands by the window. He has made an effort at mourning clothes. He is in his mid-thirties and fairly ravaged. He is taking the room in… it is very feminine, overdone… he looks totally incongruous. He is very expertly sifting behind frames and ornaments on the mantelpiece, looking to see what he might steal. Then he goes to the couch and starts searching between the cushions for coins, he finds a few and puts them in his pocket.*

KEVIN *enters and sees this. He is small, impeccably dressed in a black suit, shoes, black tie. He is trendy and neat. Both men stand silent, facing each other for a moment…*

KEVIN. They have taken her over to Smyth's.

DAMIAN. Right.

KEVIN. Noreen will make her some tea.

DAMIAN. Right… yeah.

KEVIN. I'm sure she'll be fine.

DAMIAN. Yeah.

> *Pause.* DAMIAN *shifts over towards the booze.*

> KEVIN *sits, places mass cards, keys, mobile phone on the table.*

KEVIN. How about you?

DAMIAN. Wha'?

KEVIN. Are you okay?

DAMIAN. Eh… yeah.

KEVIN. Are you sure…?

DAMIAN. Yeah… Yeah, sure… I'm all right.

KEVIN. Good.

Pause.

DAMIAN. I didn't come to fuck it up you know.

KEVIN. I'm sure.

Pause.

DAMIAN. I thought it was the right thing… comin'… I mean I thought it was the right thing to do… for Da.

KEVIN. Of course.

Pause.

DAMIAN. It's just…

KEVIN. What?

DAMIAN. Then *she* has to bleedin' start – Betty.

KEVIN *sighs*.

I mean you heard her… soon as I walked in the door…

KEVIN. Look it's all right.

DAMIAN. I didn't mean for any hassle, Kev, I swear it I…

KEVIN. Of course…

DAMIAN. It's just… this place… ya know… it just… it sets me off, it does.

KEVIN. Yes.

DAMIAN. And then she starts with the bleedin' theatrics.

KEVIN. You see I don't think she was expecting you…

DAMIAN. She wasn't wha'?

KEVIN. Try not to get worked up again, Damian.

DAMIAN. Worked up! He was me da.

KEVIN. Of course he was.

DAMIAN. Jaysus I was here before she ever was. Me and me ma were here before she ever was.

KEVIN. Of course.

DAMIAN. Before he ever married her he was me da!

KEVIN. Of course he was. It's just that this is such a difficult time… a difficult night… for everyone.

DAMIAN. Bleedin' right.

KEVIN. It's only natural to be upset.

DAMIAN. Yeah.

KEVIN. Everyone's going to be upset.

DAMIAN. Yeah… right.

KEVIN. And obviously Aunty Betty…

DAMIAN. Yeah well it's just when she started with the 'vertigo' shit and then the 'faintin''…

KEVIN. I know.

DAMIAN. It just… sets me off, Kev.

KEVIN. I know.

DAMIAN. I had to be listenin' to that for years you know.

KEVIN. I know.

DAMIAN. For years… but I didn't come here to start anything.

KEVIN. Right.

DAMIAN. I want you to know that.

KEVIN. Sure.

DAMIAN. And tell the others will ya.

KEVIN. Yes.

DAMIAN. Tell them I didn't come to start anything.

KEVIN. Great. Of course.

I will.

DAMIAN (*testing the water*). I'm gonna have another drink all right.

KEVIN. Yes. Do... do.

Pause.

It's a tense time, Damian.

DAMIAN. Tense yeah, Kev. That's what it is. Tense.

Pause.

(*Offering a drink.*) Do you want something?

KEVIN. No thanks.

DAMIAN. Sure?

KEVIN. I have the car.

DAMIAN. Yeah?

KEVIN. Can't drink and drive.

DAMIAN. Oh... Pity the old man didn't take a leaf from your book.

Awkward pause.

KEVIN. Well, they said he never came out of the coma.

DAMIAN. Yeah?

KEVIN. So he wouldn't have suffered at all.

DAMIAN. Right... good.

KEVIN. I'm sure there's some comfort in that.

DAMIAN. Yeah... comfort... yeah.

Pause.

So what's happenin'?

KEVIN. Sorry?

DAMIAN. Tonight like.

KEVIN. Tonight?

DAMIAN. Are the others comin' here from the pub?

KEVIN. Yes. I think so.

DAMIAN. Right.

He is shifting around.

For a wake thing is it?

He picks up the odd object in the room.

KEVIN. Oh yes. Yes.

DAMIAN. Right.

KEVIN. They'll be here after closing I'd imagine.

DAMIAN. Yeah... probably... after closing.

Pause.

KEVIN. It must have been a terrible shock for you.

DAMIAN. Wha'?

KEVIN. The news.

DAMIAN. Oh the news... yeah... huge... shock.

KEVIN. Terrible.

DAMIAN. Yeah.

Pause.

I never heard about the crash you know.

KEVIN. No?

DAMIAN. No.

I just met Smiley Byrne in town today, by chance it was.

KEVIN. Really?

DAMIAN. He told me.

KEVIN. Jesus.

DAMIAN. Just by chance.

KEVIN. God!

DAMIAN. Yeah.

KEVIN. You must be reeling!

DAMIAN. Reeling?!

KEVIN. In shock.

DAMIAN. Right. Yeah… all tha'.

KEVIN. That's terrible… terrible that you didn't know.

DAMIAN. And that's why I got a bit… ya know, with Betty and that.

KEVIN. Of course.

DAMIAN. I was reeling.

KEVIN. Yes.

DAMIAN. And tense.

KEVIN. Of course.

DAMIAN. So I'll just have another beer.

KEVIN. Of course.

Pause.

I think I'll have a sparkling water.

DAMIAN. What?

KEVIN. Can I have a glass of water?

DAMIAN. Oh yeah… sure… here.

As DAMIAN *delivers the glass of water he expertly slips* KEVIN*'s phone into his pocket.*

KEVIN. Thanks.

Pause.

DAMIAN. So…

KEVIN. So…

DAMIAN. How are you goin' on then?

KEVIN. Great.

DAMIAN. Yeah?

KEVIN. Not bad… busy…

DAMIAN. Yeah.

KEVIN. And you?

DAMIAN. Wha'?

KEVIN. How are you?

DAMIAN. Ehh well not great at the minute, like.

KEVIN. No. No. Of course.

    Pause.

    Are you living nearby?

DAMIAN. Wha'?

KEVIN. Are you living nearby?

DAMIAN. No… Jaysus. No.

KEVIN. I just thought you did for a while.

DAMIAN. Well I did, yeah… years ago like… up in
    Christchurch.

KEVIN. That's it.

DAMIAN. Left there ten year, easy.

KEVIN. Really.

DAMIAN. Yeah.

KEVIN. God…! Ten years.

DAMIAN. Yeah.

    You still in Rathmines then?

KEVIN. No no… not for years, either.

DAMIAN. Right…

Still in Dublin?

KEVIN. Oh yes.

Pause.

DAMIAN. In town or wha'?

KEVIN. In town… yes.

DAMIAN. Right.

Pause.

Me son's still up there.

KEVIN. Your son?

DAMIAN. Yeah. I had a son.

KEVIN. I didn't know.

DAMIAN. Yeah.

He's with his ma… up in Christchurch.

KEVIN. That's great.

DAMIAN. Yeah.

KEVIN. And how is he?

DAMIAN. Oh he's great, yeah… Chris. Chris, his name is.

KEVIN. Chris… that's great.

How old?

DAMIAN (*pause*). Ten… Twelve-ish… He's doin' great.

KEVIN. Great… fab!

DAMIAN. Yeah

Pause.

Have you kids then?

KEVIN. No.

DAMIAN. Oh, no. Right.

You workin'?

KEVIN. Yes. Yes.

DAMIAN. Great.

KEVIN. You?

DAMIAN. No

What you workin' at?

KEVIN. I'm a choreographer.

DAMIAN. Wha'?

KEVIN. A choreographer. Dance choreographer. I work in dance.

DAMIAN. Jaysus, yeah?

KEVIN. Yeah.

DAMIAN. That's gas that is!

KEVIN. Is it?

DAMIAN. Yeah. You were famous round here for it...

KEVIN. Was I?

DAMIAN. All the auld ones loved ya winnin' them Fèises.

KEVIN. Fèises! God. Yes. Well this is a lot different...

DAMIAN. I didn't know you could work at it.

KEVIN. Oh yes.

DAMIAN. Is it *Riverdance* or wha'?

KEVIN. No.

DAMIAN. What then?

KEVIN. It's contemporary dance.

DAMIAN. Oh right.

KEVIN. Yes.

DAMIAN. What's that?

KEVIN. It's... em, well I suppose it's a derivative of ballet.

DAMIAN. Oh... ballet yeah.

KEVIN. Not ballet.

DAMIAN. No?

KEVIN. No.

DAMIAN. Oh.

KEVIN. It's a modern form of dance... more in line with the body's natural form.

DAMIAN. Right.

KEVIN. And rhythm.

DAMIAN. Right.

KEVIN. It's not as rigid as ballet... more expressive.

DAMIAN. Right.

KEVIN. If that makes any sense.

DAMIAN. Oh yeah.

Pause.

KEVIN. Do you go to dance?

DAMIAN. No. Not ehhh... (*He hesitates, but so totally lost.*) no.

KEVIN. Well... I suppose it only has a small following.

DAMIAN. Like Rovers.

KEVIN. Yes. (*He laughs.*) Like Rovers.

They share the laugh.

DAMIAN. You still watch Rovers – the Hoops – then?

KEVIN. Every match.

DAMIAN. Yeah?

KEVIN. I've been to every dog-track arena and ditch.

DAMIAN. Jaysus have ya?

KEVIN. Yes.

I often wondered what had happened to you?

DAMIAN. Ya noticed?

KEVIN. Of course... we still stood with your da.

DAMIAN. Right.

KEVIN. Haven't seen you since...

DAMIAN. '95... When we lost against Bohs at the RDS.

KEVIN. Jesus.

DAMIAN. Suppose me and the Hoops hit skid row the same time.

KEVIN. Right... yes.

Pause.

And how is all that?

DAMIAN. Wha'?

KEVIN. The... well, I mean... you... how are you.

DAMIAN. Wha'?

KEVIN. In terms of the programme.

DAMIAN. What programme?

KEVIN. I thought Betty referred to your programme.

DAMIAN. Did she yeah.

KEVIN. No I just... well, it's a long time... are you through the worst or.

DAMIAN. I'm not *usin'*, like, if that's what you're askin'...

KEVIN. No no. I'm not asking!

DAMIAN. Jaysus.

KEVIN. No, I mean. I mean... I'm sorry, I don't really know what I mean. Just that you're well, I suppose that's all... are you keeping well?

DAMIAN. I'm all right.

KEVIN. Great... that's great Damian.

DAMIAN. I stick to the meths.

KEVIN. Do you... do you.

DAMIAN. Yeah...

KEVIN. Well... well done.

DAMIAN. Yeah

Gets me through... most days...

KEVIN. Great.

Pause.

Well there's been no going back that's for sure.

DAMIAN. Wha'?

KEVIN. For the Hoops... not since we lost you and the ground...

DAMIAN. Ahh right.

KEVIN. Disaster.

DAMIAN. Total.

Pause.

What's the suss with the Tallaght site?

KEVIN. Still nothing signed and sealed.

DAMIAN. Right. It's a bleedin' shambles.

KEVIN. And First Division... we never thought we'd see that!

DAMIAN. Nah… all thanks to that muppet Collins.

KEVIN. Heartbreak.

DAMIAN.…Maybe Scully'll turn it round.

KEVIN. Yeah maybe.

Pause.

Did you know your da was at the game on Saturday?!

DAMIAN. He was? Jaysus…

KEVIN. Sure of the win of course.

DAMIAN. Always the same.

Both smile.

KEVIN. Never missed a game.

DAMIAN. No?

KEVIN. No.

Pause.

DAMIAN. I still have all me *Hoops Scene*s ya know.

KEVIN. Really?

DAMIAN. Held on to fuck-all else…

Did ya ever manage to get that one from the Cup Final in '84?

KEVIN. Not a chance.

DAMIAN (*pauses*). I still have it.

KEVIN (*smiles*). Great.

DAMIAN. Kept the kit and all I did.

KEVIN. You were some player…

DAMIAN. Jaysus.

KEVIN. I remember your da the day you played under-eighteens.

DAMIAN. Yeah?

KEVIN. I thought he'd explode he was so proud.

DAMIAN. Right yeah.

KEVIN. And you played a blinder…

DAMIAN. 'Spose I was all right… yeah.

KEVIN. The Dynamo!

DAMIAN. Bleedin' Shells. Scored in the last minute…

KEVIN. The match was stolen. I remember it, we were –

DAMIAN. – gutted.

KEVIN. Yes.

DAMIAN. I got tired a losin'.

KEVIN. Well…

DAMIAN. Tired a tryin'.

Tired of the whole shaggin' lot.

He takes another drink.

KEVIN. You were some player…

DAMIAN. Right.

Pause.

KEVIN. Had you seen your da at all?

DAMIAN. Da…

KEVIN. Had you seen him recently?

DAMIAN. No.

KEVIN. Oh.

DAMIAN. Well, I don't know… maybe. Down in the village or that I can't remember… I haven't been around.

KEVIN. No.

DAMIAN. And Betty the bitch of course wouldn't let me near the house.

KEVIN. No.

DAMIAN. Not for years ya know Kev.

KEVIN. Right.

DAMIAN. Me own house.

KEVIN. Yeah.

DAMIAN. Then she has a go at me tonight like I've no right bein' here.

KEVIN. Well, she's taking it very hard Damian.

DAMIAN. I'm the one that's flesh and blood.

KEVIN. Of course.

DAMIAN. And this was me ma's gaff remember... before Big Betty ever got her arse through the door.

KEVIN *doesn't respond.*

Snook in here like a thief she did...

KEVIN. I think you should try to stay calm.

DAMIAN. Oh do ya Kev? Do ya really?

KEVIN. Look... you're angry. It's the natural reaction... the shock of your da... believe me I know how you feel, I've been through it myself.

DAMIAN. You know how I feel?!

KEVIN. I think I do...

DAMIAN. You've had it bleedin' cosy.

KEVIN. Sorry?

DAMIAN....the Leavin' Cert... the lunch box... the DIT.

KEVIN. What?

DAMIAN. You always had the best goin'... even from school.

KEVIN. School!

DAMIAN. Bikes and Scalextric, you had it all you did.

KEVIN. I mean...

DAMIAN. I got bleedin' Betty, Kev...! Betty and her Mr Sheen... she came in scrubbin' till she just rubbed the rest of us out.

KEVIN *sighs*.

KEVIN. I just meant... I've been through it too.

DAMIAN. Through fuckin' wha'?

KEVIN. Death. I've been through death. The death of a parent.

DAMIAN. Oh... that.

KEVIN. Yes. That. Both parents in fact.

DAMIAN. Right.

KEVIN. And it's not easy.

DAMIAN. No.

KEVIN. It's like the ground goes from under you.

DAMIAN. Yeah.

KEVIN. So I understand, that's what I meant.

DAMIAN. Oh... right.

KEVIN. Nothing can prepare you for it.

DAMIAN *doesn't reply*.

Shattering... isn't it.

He earnestly awaits a reaction.

DAMIAN. Oh... yeah.

KEVIN. I mean your whole sense of security, certainty... it's just shattered isn't it. I know it, Damian. I know.

DAMIAN. Right.

KEVIN. It's just so final… so… God.

DAMIAN. Jaysus…

KEVIN (*realising this might not be the appropriate line*).

But then time, Damian, TIME is the great healer.

No response.

I know it's hard to accept it now… tonight… but believe me, one day, you'll wake up and it'll be all right.

DAMIAN. Yeah.

KEVIN. The sun WILL shine.

DAMIAN *just throws him a look.*

Well it'll be okay…

Pause.

DAMIAN. I'm sorry they died.

KEVIN. Thanks. Thank you.

DAMIAN. I didn't know.

KEVIN. No.

They both sit in silence.

DAMIAN. Did they leave ya the gaff?

KEVIN. What?

DAMIAN. The gaff in Ballyroan… did you get it?

KEVIN. Well, yes, of course.

DAMIAN. Right.

KEVIN. Jesus.

DAMIAN. Wha'?

KEVIN. What?

DAMIAN. What do ya mean 'Jesus'?

KEVIN. Well…

DAMIAN. Well just have a look at what I bleedin' get!

KEVIN. Is that what this is about?

DAMIAN. Wha'?

KEVIN. Is that why you're here?

DAMIAN. Wha'?

KEVIN. To see what you can get?

DAMIAN. No… it's not why I'm here.

KEVIN. Then why bring it up?

DAMIAN. Coz… coz it's easy for you… it's easy when everything's dished out to ya.

KEVIN (*knowingly*). Oh right.

DAMIAN. I've had to fight me corner with that bitch since I was a kid and for wha'…? Nothin', would ya look at this place, it's like me and me ma never existed… there's nothin' of us… and now me da's gone… it's like… it's like I'M nothin'.

Pause.

I just feel… I just feel I'm entitled to something Kev… well at least to bleedin' be here.

KEVIN. Right.

Yes.

DAMIAN. It's all such… such a waste ya know.

KEVIN. Is it?

DAMIAN. It's like everything was fucked from the start.

Me ma, wiped…

KEVIN. I know… That was tragic I…

DAMIAN. And she was just a kid… I was thinking of that on the bus over… twenty-two she was.

KEVIN. God.

DAMIAN. And we used to go on the bus…

No response.

Me and me ma.

KEVIN. Yes… right.

DAMIAN. And I was thinkin' that. Thinking of that on the bus.

KEVIN. Well yes… of course.

DAMIAN. Her ma lived in the barn, we'd get the sixteen to Harold's Cross.

KEVIN. Ahh yes.

DAMIAN. Walk down the canal.

KEVIN. Yeah.

DAMIAN. I remember that.

KEVIN. Do you?

Well that's great… great.

DAMIAN. I remember sittin' up front… them big gates at the village… part of the castle, do ya remember them before the new road?

KEVIN. Ehh… I'm not sure.

DAMIAN. Well they were there.

KEVIN. Oh right.

DAMIAN. And it was her.

KEVIN. Yes.

DAMIAN. On the bus… goin' down the barn… with me.

KEVIN. Lovely.

DAMIAN. I was thinking it all again.

KEVIN. Were you… yes?

DAMIAN. I can even hear her change rattling... chhhk. Ding comes the ticket... yeah!

Pause.

I know it was her. That close... on me seat...

Pause.

KEVIN. I'm so sorry, Damian.

No response from DAMIAN.

Tragic.

DAMIAN. Yeah well... them's the breaks.

KEVIN. Yes.

Yes.

DAMIAN. And not a sign of her here, of course... not a picture... your Betty made sure of that.

No response.

A waste.

KEVIN. She might not see it that way.

I mean there's you...

DAMIAN. I'm a waste... and Da! What does he do... finally mows himself into a tree... and that's it... that's just the end of it.

KEVIN. There's Chris?!

DAMIAN *gives him a look and drinks.*

Pause.

This... this is the dark time, Damian, but there's plenty of time... time to move on.

DAMIAN. Yeah.

KEVIN. I mean we've all got to look to the future...

DAMIAN. Wha'?

KEVIN. It's no good dragging through the past.

DAMIAN. And what would you know about it?

KEVIN. I'm only sayin'.

DAMIAN. Well don't say. Right.

You've no idea... no idea what it was like livin' here.

KEVIN. I'm sure...

DAMIAN. Sure of what, Kev...? Sure that I was a bleedin' menace... a scrounger... the junkie-thief?!

KEVIN. No...

DAMIAN. Betty always had your ear... you and your ma... just like she had Da's... had Da's from the day she moved in.

KEVIN. But this isn't about Betty.

DAMIAN. Well what is it about...? What is the whole thing about Kev?

KEVIN. I don't know... I don't pretend to know... But what I do know is that it always helps to talk.

DAMIAN. So... talk.

KEVIN. A good counsellor...

DAMIAN. Jaysus.

KEVIN. I found mine a lifeline after Mammy...

DAMIAN. I've been listenin' to those morons for years.

KEVIN. But.

DAMIAN. And they solve nothing, not the gear... not this shit... nothin'.

KEVIN. I don't agree.

DAMIAN. Well I don't give a shit...

KEVIN. Maybe this just isn't a good time.

DAMIAN. There are no good times.

He gets another drink.

Pause.

KEVIN. Do you know that the Jews actually legislate for grief.

DAMIAN. The what? The Jews? What are you talking about?

KEVIN. Under Jewish law you're entitled to three days descent to the depths, seven days to mourn and then slowly you're expected to return to the living.

DAMIAN. Right.

KEVIN. So maybe I can call you in a week!

DAMIAN. I don't think so.

A brief pause.

KEVIN. They have a tradition. Called the Kriah. The Jews.

No response.

They rip their clothes.

DAMIAN. Wha'?

KEVIN. The mourners… they literally wrench the cloth… it is seen as a symbolic gesture to express the grief within…

DAMIAN. Right… great… who gives a toss.

KEVIN. I used it in my show.

DAMIAN *doesn't react.*

My last dance show *Grief.*

DAMIAN. Your wha'?

KEVIN. Well after the folks and that… I was reeling.

DAMIAN. Oh reeling again is it?

KEVIN. So I thought it might be interesting to explore family bereavement through dance.

DAMIAN. Ya did?

KEVIN. And the Kriah really worked?

DAMIAN. Right.

KEVIN. We used these two dancers and a corpse.

DAMIAN. Ya did.

KEVIN. And they started this shredding… slowly at first… then kind of frantic… tearing, ripping… reefing at their clothes.

DAMIAN. Two birds was it?

KEVIN. No.

DAMIAN. Oh.

KEVIN. But it really said it… you know… it really demonstrated that pain.

DAMIAN. Right.

KEVIN. Oh yes. Fascinating…

Pause.

DAMIAN. Show us a bit, so?

KEVIN. What?

DAMIAN. Show us a bit of the dance.

KEVIN. The dance?

DAMIAN. Yeah.

KEVIN. Oh no. No you see I don't actually dance myself.

DAMIAN. Don't ya?

KEVIN. No… I invent it…

DAMIAN. Ya used to dance.

KEVIN. Yes, but not now… I injured my knees.

DAMIAN. The both of them.

KEVIN. They've never been the same since *Annie*.

DAMIAN. Ahhhhh right.

Well it sounded good… *the rippin'*.

KEVIN. Yes… it was. I think people were really affected by it…

DAMIAN. Right.

Pause.

Just show us a bit of it.

KEVIN. It won't make any sense.

DAMIAN. Sure, what would I know?

KEVIN. Well I suppose I could give you an idea.

DAMIAN. Great.

KEVIN. Of how it worked. But just an idea.

DAMIAN. Right.

KEVIN. It will look a bit odd now… totally out of context.

DAMIAN. Grand.

KEVIN. And remember I didn't perform it myself.

DAMIAN. Would ya go on?

KEVIN. Right. Okay.

He gets into position.

Now imagine colour.

DAMIAN. Yeah.

KEVIN. Vivid colour.

DAMIAN. Yeah.

KEVIN. And two small broken black figures emerge.

He starts to move into the space.

DAMIAN. Yeah.

KEVIN. The colour drains to grey as they take up position.

DAMIAN. Oh yeah.

KEVIN. Bleak… shadow… hurt.

He breaks into a slow Kriah dance routine (but with no ripping here) perhaps some keening – but not too ham!

When he finishes…

DAMIAN. That was famous that was.

KEVIN. Phew!

DAMIAN. It was, Kev. Somethin' else!

KEVIN. Thanks. I can't imagine what it looked like.

DAMIAN. Where'd ya learn it?

KEVIN. What?

DAMIAN. That dancin'.

KEVIN. It's well... it just develops I suppose... you know...
through years of work.

DAMIAN. Great.

KEVIN. Thanks. I must say, it feels great.

DAMIAN. Does it?

KEVIN. Just to fucking express...

DAMIAN. Yeah?

KEVIN. To work it out Damian... work through that emotion...
I mean it comes from deep within doesn't it... the loss?

DAMIAN. Loss.

KEVIN. There's more than one way to release it.

DAMIAN. 'Spose.

So have ya really made it then?

KEVIN. Made it?

DAMIAN. With the dancing...

KEVIN. Well I don't know, that depends... I'm doing well...
I'm in work...

DAMIAN. Yeah.

That was good. What ya did.

KEVIN. Thanks.

DAMIAN. I could see ya get the buzz.

KEVIN. Right.

DAMIAN. Flyin'.

KEVIN. Yes.

   Thanks.

DAMIAN (*with a smile*). You're gas.

   Pause.

KEVIN. The worst thing you can do is repress.

   DAMIAN*'s not interested*.

   Damian.

DAMIAN. Wha'?

KEVIN. Repress!

DAMIAN. Wha'?

KEVIN. Your mother?

   No response.

   We all have to grieve…

DAMIAN. Yeah.

KEVIN. We've got to grieve first… and then we can move on.

DAMIAN. Right.

KEVIN. Your mother's death…

DAMIAN. Yeah, yeah.

KEVIN. And Betty's arrival…

DAMIAN. Oh, fuck this.

KEVIN. No don't turn away.

DAMIAN. Just drop it now.

KEVIN. But you can't deny your feelings.

DAMIAN. Will ya leave it.

KEVIN. But…

DAMIAN. I've heard it all before, Kev… been through it all before, right, and it doesn't change nothing… it doesn't do fuck-all… so drop it… drop it now, yeah?

KEVIN. Okay… okay.

Sorry.

Pause.

It's just… I'd like to help.

DAMIAN. I don't need your help.

KEVIN. Right.

DAMIAN. What I need is a bit of space.

KEVIN. Right.

DAMIAN. Me head is wrecked.

KEVIN. Of course.

DAMIAN. Yeah.

KEVIN. Of course.

Pause.

It's just… I do have the name of an excellent counsellor.

DAMIAN. Jaysus.

KEVIN. It's a very holistic approach.

DAMIAN. Would ya give it a rest.

KEVIN. Look I know you think I had it easy.

DAMIAN *sighs.*

But I've lost.

DAMIAN. I just want to have a drink for me da.

KEVIN. We've all lost.

DAMIAN. Right. We've lost. Grand. Can we just leave it at that.

KEVIN. I don't know anyone... anyone, Damian, untouched by grief... It's how you deal with it that matters.

DAMIAN. Right. Grand.

He drinks.

KEVIN. I mean look at me.

DAMIAN. Oh, you.

KEVIN. I have felt weighed down... all my life.

DAMIAN *gives him a quizzical look.*

Weighed down by love.

DAMIAN. Wha'?

KEVIN. Well I was the only child.

I was the future... For Mam and Dad I was all aspiration. Can you imagine the pressure of that...

DAMIAN. Oh, brutal that, yeah...

KEVIN. Don't mock, Damian, please. You've no idea... every move was marked... every moment leaden with that... with that... love.

DAMIAN *can think of no reply.*

And I hated it. Hated them.

DAMIAN. You hated your ma?

KEVIN. Yes.

DAMIAN. But youse were... close

KEVIN. Exactly.

DAMIAN. Very close... and Betty... youse were all close.

KEVIN. Exactly. Suffocating.

DAMIAN. Right.

KEVIN. And now they're gone.

DAMIAN. Gone.

KEVIN. Gone.

DAMIAN. Oh right.

KEVIN. So that's the end of it.

DAMIAN. Yeah.

Pause.

KEVIN. But I'm still here… still living.

DAMIAN. Yeah.

KEVIN. And you.

DAMIAN. Just about…

KEVIN. So we've got to live… we've got to love… to move on.

DAMIAN *looks at him.*

Pause.

The counselling helps.

DAMIAN. Not for me.

KEVIN. Family helps.

DAMIAN *snorts.*

DAMIAN. I might as well bleedin' dance as go lookin' to them.

KEVIN. So… dance.

DAMIAN *looks at him and laughs.*

Why not?

DAMIAN. Why not?

KEVIN. Why not?

They face each other as if in a duel.

DAMIAN. All right.

Give us a go.

KEVIN. You'll dance?

DAMIAN. Fuck it.

KEVIN. Right.

DAMIAN. Right.

KEVIN. And you're not messin'?

DAMIAN. No.

KEVIN. Right.

DAMIAN. Right.

    You show us it again and I'll follow ya.

KEVIN. The Kriah!

DAMIAN. Whatever.

KEVIN. Kriah.

DAMIAN. Right.

    This is the night for it.

    He takes a final swig and gets into position.

KEVIN. You need to be on my left.

DAMIAN. Okay.

KEVIN. We'll keep it simple to start.

DAMIAN. Okay.

KEVIN. Then you move with me.

DAMIAN. Copy ya.

KEVIN. Mirror.

DAMIAN. Right.

KEVIN. Imagine colour.

DAMIAN. Skip the shit and show me, will ya.

KEVIN. Okay... okay. Now start with the head... slowly...
    yes... good and follow me... good, Damian.

And so he teaches DAMIAN *the sequence. They repeat the initial movements a few times before getting to the ripping stage. Then they do rip… rip and rip the shirts off each other and into tatters. They laugh until they are sitting.*

Then they are silent for a time.

You know I have to ask you to leave.

Pause.

Damian…

DAMIAN. Yeah… I know.

KEVIN. I'm sorry.

DAMIAN. Right.

KEVIN. It's just Betty…

DAMIAN. Yeah.

KEVIN. She can't have you here.

DAMIAN. No.

KEVIN. Too much water under the bridge.

DAMIAN. Yeah.

KEVIN. Sorry.

DAMIAN. It's all right.

KEVIN. She said you could come to the church.

DAMIAN. Did she…?

KEVIN. The mass is at ten in the morning. In the village.

DAMIAN. Yeah.

DAMIAN *drinks.* KEVIN *is silent.*

I remember nothin' of me ma.

KEVIN. No.

DAMIAN. And now there's no going back with Da…

KEVIN. No.

DAMIAN. I'm sorry about that.

KEVIN. Yes.

Pause.

DAMIAN *makes to leave.*

DAMIAN. I'll let ya get on with it.

He returns the mobile phone to the table. KEVIN *has never noticed him taking it and does not notice its return.*

KEVIN. Damian.

DAMIAN. Yeah.

KEVIN (*beat*). You'll come to the church?

DAMIAN (*beat*). Nah.

DAMIAN *leaves.*

The End.

BOGBOY

Bogboy was first performed at Solstice Arts Centre, Meath, on 19 June 2010. The cast was as follows:

HUGHIE DOLAN   Steve Blount
DARREN   Emmet Kirwan
BRIGIT   Mary Murry
ANNIE   Noelle Brown

Director   Jo Mangan
Producer   Tracy Martin
Costumes   Elaine Chapman
Music   Philip Stewart
Film Cast   Padraig Loughran
Film Cast   Shay Carry
Film Cast   David Halleran
Film Cast   Philip Brady
Stage Manager   Emma Hannon
Assistant Stage Manager   Georgina Ricotti
Graphic Designer   Karen Madsen
Designer   Ciaran Bagnall
Publicity Photography   Patrick Redmond
AV Operator   Duncan Malloy

Characters

BRIGIT, *about thirty, from Dublin*
HUGHIE DOLAN, *mid-fifties, from rural Meath*
DARREN, *Brigit's ex-boyfriend, from Dublin*
ANNIE, *Brigit's social worker, from Dublin*

Scene One

Present.

We are in a drug drop-in centre. BRIGIT *sits alone on a chair.* ANNIE *passes her by, busy.* ANNIE *stops and returns.*

ANNIE. Brigit?

BRIGIT. Oh howaya, Annie.

ANNIE. I was just thinking about you this morning.

BRIGIT. Oh were ya yeah?

ANNIE. I was down in Meath.

Well I was at the café… the café in Navan… I don't know if you remember…

BRIGIT. Of course I remember.

I'm fucked but not senile…

ANNIE. No.

Well.

I just thought of you because… Hughie… that man… the neighbour, I don't know, do you remember Hughie?

BRIGIT. What did I just tell ya?

I remember Navan.

I remember Hughie.

ANNIE. That's him.

Well…

BRIGIT. Well what?

ANNIE. He died.

BRIGIT. Hughie?

ANNIE. Yes.

BRIGIT. Oh.

ANNIE. I'm sorry. I don't know why but I thought that you were… I know it was years ago but when I heard about him… such a sad end. I thought of you… that you and he were once.

BRIGIT. Friends.

ANNIE. Yes.

Friends.

You were.

BRIGIT. We were.

ANNIE. Well. I'm sorry. I saw you and I just thought I'd tell you.

BRIGIT. Right. Thanks.

ANNIE. Yes.

BRIGIT. Poor Hughie.

ANNIE. Yes.

BRIGIT. What he die of?

ANNIE. Oh… He was at home. He was… well… I think it was his liver… his age.

BRIGIT. Loneliness.

ANNIE. Well.

Maybe.

It was certainly a while before they found him.

BRIGIT. Of course it was.

Poor fucker.

ANNIE. He was in his chair apparently…

BRIGIT. For weeks?

ANNIE. I think so… yes… for a while at any rate.

BRIGIT. Rotten…

ANNIE. Yes.

I suppose.

It is.

Slight pause.

And how are you doing Brigit?

BRIGIT. Shite.

ANNIE. Oh.

On the methadone?

BRIGIT. On the fucking methadone.

ANNIE. Well that's good.

BRIGIT. Is it?

ANNIE. It'll give you a chance.

BRIGIT. For what exactly?

ANNIE. Well.

Pause.

Where are you living now?

BRIGIT. The shelter.

ANNIE. Oh.

Pause.

I best get back.

BRIGIT. You best.

ANNIE. It's good to see you Brigit.

No reply.

ANNIE *returns to her office. She sits at her desk.*

BRIGIT *has watched her go. She now gets off her chair and follows her.*

BRIGIT. Annie!

ANNIE. You know you are not allowed in here Brigit.

BRIGIT. I know.

I just… I'm sorry… I just thought I'd write a letter.

ANNIE. A letter?

BRIGIT. For Hughie.

ANNIE. Oh.

BRIGIT. For Hughie… for… I don't know.

Just… I better do it now while the mood is on me, coz… you know me.

Once I go. I'm gone.

ANNIE. A letter?

BRIGIT. Yeah.

Can I write it here… I thought maybe I could write it here.

I won't rob anything.

ANNIE. But I'm not… you know I can't have you in here, Brigit.

BRIGIT. I'm not after anything.

Honest.

I'm trying to do something here. For Hughie.

Just sit there. Sit there Annie and don't move. I'll sit here. I'll write it and I'll be gone.

ANNIE. A letter?

BRIGIT. Yeah.

ANNIE. To his family?

BRIGIT. No, he didn't have one.

This is to someone... someone else.

ANNIE. I don't know, Brigit.

BRIGIT. I'll be ten minutes.

It's important. It's something good.

I think I can do something good.

ANNIE. Well.

Okay.

Okay Brigit, you can sit there.

But I've got my eye on you.

BRIGIT. I won't nick a thing. Promise.

Except maybe the pen!

Joking...! I'm joking, Annie...

Lights change. We move now out of reality and into the letter and BRIGIT*'s memory.*

BRIGIT *stands front to deliver the letter. She looks out front.*

Scene Two

BRIGIT *narrates her letter.*

BRIGIT. Dear Mrs... Dear Bernie... no, dear Bernadette Robins. I am writin'... I am writin' coz I want to tell you about me friend... a friend... Hughie Dolan. He knew your brother... your brother Gerard.

I know it's bad that I'm only writin' now... I know you must be thinkin'... thinkin' maybe I'm a spoofer... I suppose there's been loads of spoofers over the years but this one is real Mrs Robins... Bernie. Ya see I used to live in Meath, not far from, well in it really – your Gerard's bog. I was on a placement and I worked in Navan and... well it's a long story.

HUGHIE *comes out on stage.* BRIGIT *pauses and watches him, remembering.* BRIGIT *continues with the letter.*

The thing is, I was there when they were lookin' for Gerard... the police. When they were diggin' in the bog and I know they never found him and I was real sorry about that. I was sorry for you and for him... layin' there and the thing is Bernie, me friend Hughie, he told me you see, he told me one night, all about your Gerard and he wanted me to help... but I didn't.

I didn't. And the thing is, maybe now I can... coz I know where Gerard's buried, Bernie, and I'd like to help, if it's not too late... for Hughie, ya see, I'd like to help him bring your brother home.

Scene Three

BRIGIT *leaves the letter. She stands as if waiting for a lift.* HUGHIE *approaches.*

HUGHIE. Howaya!

BRIGIT. Wha'?

HUGHIE. How are ye?

BRIGIT. What the fuck do ye want?

HUGHIE. Hah?

BRIGIT. Sneakin' up on me like that.

HUGHIE. Hah?

BRIGIT. You could kill someone like that.

Give them a heart attack.

HUGHIE. But this is my gate.

BRIGIT. Oh is it. Is it mister? And is it a crime to be standing here is it? At your fuckin' gate.

Poor HUGHIE *is nonplussed as she turns her back on him.*

HUGHIE. Well I thought you might be wantin' a lift?

BRIGIT. Wha'?

HUGHIE. I thought. Well it's just ya look like ya might be wantin' a lift.

BRIGIT. So...?

HUGHIE. Well I could give ya one.

BRIGIT. Oh, could ya now?

HUGHIE. Yes.

BRIGIT. And ya think I just get into any looper's car?

HUGHIE. Hah?

BRIGIT. Would ya get lost?

She turns from him in disdain. He hovers, not quite sure what has happened. He slopes away.

She remains standing, there is not a car in sight.

HUGHIE *comes back in a car. This can be created cinematically or in accordance with the director's view of the style of the piece.*

HUGHIE. I'm goin' into Navan.

BRIGIT. Are ya now.

HUGHIE. Aye. Is that where you're headed.

BRIGIT. It is actually.

HUGHIE. Right.

BRIGIT. Yeah.

HUGHIE. Would ya like to hop in so?

BRIGIT sighs.

BRIGIT. All right. All right.

She gets in.

HUGHIE. It's a cold morning.

BRIGIT. It is yeah… Freezin'.

HUGHIE. I'll turn up the heating.

She watches his hand like a shark, he is oblivious.

She relaxes a bit.

He smiles.

BRIGIT. Thanks.

HUGHIE. No bother.

BRIGIT. Yeah.

Snuffles.

It's the cold.

HUGHIE. Oh aye.

Pause.

BRIGIT. So you're headin' into Navan?

HUGHIE. I am.

BRIGIT. Great.

HUGHIE. Yeah.

BRIGIT. And ya live in that house is it?

HUGHIE. Yeah.

BRIGIT. Right.

HUGHIE. Not far from ya.

BRIGIT. What?

HUGHIE. Not far from you.

BRIGIT. No.

Not quite comfortable with him knowing where she lives.

No.

HUGHIE. You're in a grand spot.

BRIGIT *laughs*.

BRIGIT. A what? Are ya fuckin' jokin' me?

HUGHIE. Hah?

BRIGIT. It's a wilderness it is.

HUGHIE. Hah?

BRIGIT. A bleedin' wilderness. I mean there's not a bus!

HUGHIE. No.

BRIGIT. And ya never see a sinner walkin' round. No one, no one and nothin'. Except fuckin' cows. Maybe you're supposed to ride them into work.

HUGHIE. Are you going into work?

BRIGIT. I am. I am believe it or not. But how I'm supposed to get there I don't know. It's bleedin' ridiculous!

HUGHIE. Is it?

BRIGIT. And I said as much to me worker.

HUGHIE. Did you?

BRIGIT. Yeah.

Pause.

HUGHIE. Your worker?

BRIGIT. Me social worker. ME SOCIAL WORKER!

HUGHIE. Oh right.

BRIGIT. I'm a placement mister, I'm on rehab.

HUGHIE. Oh.

BRIGIT. It's all right. I don't mind tellin' ya. Because it's part of me therapy you see, to say it like it is coz I've been in denial for years.

HUGHIE. Oh right.

BRIGIT. And I mean I'm all for this startin' afresh like to keep clean. I've no problem with any of that but the bog is fuckin' third world it is...

HUGHIE. Is it?

BRIGIT. Well yeah!

HUGHIE. Oh.

BRIGIT. I mean it's all right for the likes of you... obviously... but I'm used to a bit of life around me ya know... *Civilisation*. And all right Navan's a kip but at least there's people in it, ya know what I mean?

HUGHIE. Oh there is that.

BRIGIT. I mean what are they at mister? Can ya tell me that? Havin' me live in the middle of nowhere, does that make any sense... does it?

HUGHIE. Ehhh... no... no.

BRIGIT. I think it's abuse, meself, that's what I said to me worker.

HUGHIE. Did you?

BRIGIT. Abuse.

HUGHIE. Right.

And what did he say?

BRIGIT. Ahh the usual shite about isolatin' meself and that... moving away from old habits... new *environment*.

I think they're just savin' money on the rent.

HUGHIE. Is that a fact?

BRIGIT. I mean the job is in Navan. And they're the ones set it up. Why have me livin' in a bog six mile away, does that make any sense?

HUGHIE. Oh aye... no, no sense at all.

BRIGIT. No.

It's left here for the shoppin' centre.

HUGHIE. Oh it is, eh, right so.

BRIGIT. What?

HUGHIE. Eh?

BRIGIT. Were ya not goin' that way?

HUGHIE. No, I was goin' up to the hospital.

BRIGIT. Well ya should have said.

HUGHIE. I suppose.

BRIGIT. Is there something wrong with ya?

HUGHIE. No...

BRIGIT. Tests is it?

HUGHIE. No...

BRIGIT. Something serious?

HUGHIE. No... no...

BRIGIT. I'm just here, thanks.

HUGHIE. Oh right.

BRIGIT. I work in the caff, I do... in the shopping centre.

HUGHIE. Ahhh.

BRIGIT. So, thanks for the lift.

HUGHIE. Ahh no bother I...

BRIGIT. I'll see ya.

HUGHIE. Right… sure…

She hops out of the car and walks away.

Bye.

Scene Four

BRIGIT *returns to writing her letter.*

BRIGIT. I couldn't see it at first, Bernie, but it's a beautiful place your Gerard's bog… low and brown but living, if ya know what I mean?

I got to know it proper when I started painting, Bernie; I grew to love the white cotton like breath blowin' up… and the big bog holes seeping. Seeping like this is the place where the world opens up, opens up and sighs. I mean I know he's fierce far from home, Gerard. Far from the clamour of Belfast… I missed Dublin meself when I was there but it's not the worst, Bernie… it's not the worst place for him to lie.

It is another day and BRIGIT *arrives at* HUGHIE's *gate.*

Ahh howaya, it's you.

HUGHIE. It is.

BRIGIT. Did you get the results of them tests then?

HUGHIE. Hah?

BRIGIT. At the hospital the other day.

HUGHIE. Ahhh… no… no.

BRIGIT. So what's the story then?

HUGHIE. Story?

BRIGIT. Well what did they tell ya – are ya sick or what?

HUGHIE. Oh no. No I'm grand.

BRIGIT. Are ya sure?

HUGHIE. Yes.

BRIGIT. Coz ya don't look great.

HUGHIE. No?

BRIGIT. No... I mean I know I don't know ya or anything but I wasn't a bit surprised the last day like that you were goin' to the hospital coz you're pasty you know... yellow, even.

HUGHIE. Yellow?

BRIGIT. Round the eyes...

HUGHIE. Really?

BRIGIT. Yeah.

HUGHIE. But I wasn't...

I do a bit of paintin' at the hospital.

BRIGIT. Oh, do ya?

HUGHIE. Yes.

BRIGIT. Well then you've no excuse.

HUGHIE. No?

BRIGIT. For not gettin' yourself checked. I mean you're on site.

HUGHIE. Oh, I suppose I am.

Pause.

BRIGIT. I do a bit of paintin' meself.

HUGHIE. Do you?

BRIGIT. Yeah... art like.

HUGHIE. Marvellous.

BRIGIT. Adult education, there's a VEC by the river there in Navan.

HUGHIE. There is.

BRIGIT. Does all sorts of courses.

HUGHIE. Does it now?

BRIGIT. Annie reckons it's good for me to have a pastime while I'm here like. Annie's me social worker… she's a bit of a meddler but she's all right. Anyway she got me the leaflet and I took up art.

HUGHIE. Well isn't that marvellous.

BRIGIT. Yeah. It's all right.

So what kind of paintin' are you doin' then?

HUGHIE. Walls…

BRIGIT. Oh.

Right.

Pause.

So do you be goin' into Navan every day then?

HUGHIE. No. I'd only be called into the hospital the odd time, for maintenance or that.

BRIGIT. Right.

I was only askin'.

HUGHIE. Of course.

Pause.

BRIGIT. Though I'm not havin' much luck with the lift, like.

HUGHIE. Oh aye.

Pause.

Would ya not think of getting a bike?

BRIGIT. A bike?!

HUGHIE. Sure you're only five mile out from Navan.

BRIGIT. And what would I be doin' on a bike? I never had one in me life!

HUGHIE. You never had a bike?

BRIGIT. Nooo. Jaysus.

HUGHIE. Well I have an old one out the back…

BRIGIT. I mean me brother had a bike all right.

He used it for courierin'!

HUGHIE. Ya see, good man.

BRIGIT. Drugs… for courierin' drugs, mister.

HUGHIE. Oh.

Pause.

BRIGIT. So what's with your bike then?

HUGHIE. It's an old one. Me mother's.

BRIGIT. Jaysus.

HUGHIE. It goes grand… and sure you're welcome to it.

BRIGIT. Me?

HUGHIE. Aye. I could get ya started if ya like.

BRIGIT. What?

HUGHIE. Teach ya.

BRIGIT. Teach me?

HUGHIE. Aye.

BRIGIT. Really?

HUGHIE. Well it's no bother…

BRIGIT. No?

HUGHIE. No.

Pause.

BRIGIT. Suppose it's not as daft as it seems.

HUGHIE. No, no.

BRIGIT. Better than this walkin' up to the pub and waitin' for the Navan bus.

HUGHIE. Exactly.

BRIGIT. And it doesn't come half the time.

HUGHIE. No.

BRIGIT. And I'm sick of hitchin'.

HUGHIE. Exactly.

Pause.

BRIGIT. It's not some kind of a pervy thing ya have goin' is it?

HUGHIE. What?

BRIGIT. With me?

HUGHIE. What?

BRIGIT. And a bike.

HUGHIE. What?

BRIGIT. Well I have to ask.

Pause.

Being a girl on me own, like.

HUGHIE. Oh right.

BRIGIT. Grand.

HUGHIE. Grand.

BRIGIT. Thanks.

HUGHIE. Sure.

BRIGIT. But I could do with a lift now so I could.

HUGHIE. Oh.

BRIGIT. Or I'll miss me shift.

HUGHIE. Oh right.

BRIGIT. Would ya mind?

HUGHIE. No no. I'll get the car.

BRIGIT. Sure you could do a bit of shoppin' maybe.

HUGHIE. I could.

BRIGIT. Then come into the caff and I'll look after you for lunch.

HUGHIE. No need.

BRIGIT. Ahh, go on, it's me thank-you...

HUGHIE. Well I will, so.

BRIGIT. For the lift... and the bike!

HUGHIE. Hah?

BRIGIT. Coz I might just take you up on that...

HUGHIE. Will ya...?

BRIGIT. Brigit.

HUGHIE. Brigit.

BRIGIT. And what's your name then?

HUGHIE. Hughie.

Hughie Dolan.

BRIGIT. Great, thanks then Hughie.

HUGHIE. No bother.

HUGHIE *exits*.

Scene Five

BRIGIT *returns to the letter.*

BRIGIT. He lived next door to me, Hughie. Well as next door as ya get down there. His family were from Donegal so he was a blow-in of forty-eight years. To me he seemed total 'culchie' but now I think of it, I think he was as much outside of Meath as me.

I want to tell you about him Bernie coz, well, he just wasn't a bad man. I mean we all do some shit in life but it doesn't mean we're all bad... does it? Hughie was really, he was really, he was all right – he did odd jobs around me house and he took an interest ya know, in me life, and not coz he wanted anythin' no... just coz... well... coz.

HUGHIE *comes in with an old black bike.* BRIGIT *leaves her letter and joins the memory.*

HUGHIE. Here she is, now don't stop pedalling this time.

BRIGIT. I didn't stop pedallin', it was a bleedin' pothole.

HUGHIE. Well just go round it.

BRIGIT. Oh that's easy for you to say but I was fuckin' in it before I seen it.

He gives her a push and she pedals off.

HUGHIE. Keep your eyes on what's ahead of ya.

BRIGIT. See ya sucker!

She falls.

HUGHIE. Jesus tonight.

BRIGIT. I'm grand.

HUGHIE. Are ya hurted?

BRIGIT. No, I just got the wobbles again.

HUGHIE. You've to keep pedalling. You're balancing grand you know.

BRIGIT. Doesn't feel like it and I think somethin' crunched on me...

HUGHIE. Ahh it's just the chain, easy fixed.

BRIGIT. I loved it though Hughie. I was flyin' the first time wasn't I?

HUGHIE. You were, you were Brigit.

BRIGIT. It's a gas feelin' isn't it... steamin' along.

HUGHIE. Sure you're a natural.

BRIGIT. Yeah.

HUGHIE. Hop off and I'll fix that chain.

BRIGIT. Jaysus, I'd love to do this with Kaylie.

HUGHIE. Kaylie?

BRIGIT. Me daughter… I'd love to teach her somethin' just like this exactly the same as us now…

HUGHIE. You've a daughter?

BRIGIT. Yeah.

HUGHIE. Sure why not!

BRIGIT. They do have lovely bikes for kids.

HUGHIE. I'm sure they do.

BRIGIT. I'll have to wait till she starts walking of course then maybe get her one of them little trikes, do ya know them Hughie?

HUGHIE. Can't say I do.

BRIGIT. I never knew you could have so much craic at it.

HUGHIE. Well I have to hand it to you, you learnt fast.

BRIGIT. I did, didn't I.

HUGHIE. Fair play.

BRIGIT. I might get a visit with her soon ya know.

HUGHIE. Who?

BRIGIT. Kaylie!

HUGHIE. A visit?

BRIGIT. Yeah.

HUGHIE. Sure that's grand

BRIGIT. She's eleven months, she is.

HUGHIE. Eleven months, God save us.

BRIGIT. I know. Tiny. I'd love to get to see her Hughie… She's, well she was taken away.

HUGHIE. From her mother?

BRIGIT. It'd be a supervised visit, I'm trying to get Annie to swing it for me on account of me doing so well on the programme.

HUGHIE. I see.

BRIGIT. She says I'm doin' great.

HUGHIE. Great.

BRIGIT. She says I'm really focused.

HUGHIE. Does she?

BRIGIT. Yeah. I haven't slipped once.

HUGHIE. Well fair play to you.

BRIGIT. She might ask Darren to bring her down. Darren's her da… Kaylie's with her da.

HUGHIE. Oh.

BRIGIT. So I'm hoping, ya know?

HUGHIE. Well of course you are.

BRIGIT. But I don't like it Hughie, I can tell you that. I don't like hoping.

HUGHIE. Do you not?

BRIGIT. No. Hoping is bleedin' terrifying.

HUGHIE. I suppose it can be.

BRIGIT. I mean she's the only reason I'm doin' this, Kaylie is.

HUGHIE. Is she?

BRIGIT. I couldn't give a toss about meself Hughie and that's the truth. But with Kaylie like… I feel I got a second chance.

HUGHIE. At what?

BRIGIT. At everything. At life, I mean you didn't know me before, Hughie… I'm a disaster.

HUGHIE. No.

BRIGIT. I am, I'm tellin' ya…

HUGHIE. How?

BRIGIT. Everyhow that's how. But with Kaylie I'm different. I am. There's been a few slip-ups you know yourself but I mean I stayed off the smack and all when I was pregnant… No one could believe it… Couldn't believe it meself…

HUGHIE. No?

BRIGIT. Then I blew it of course, like always but… I'm getting back on track now and that's what matters.

HUGHIE. It is. It is Brigit.

BRIGIT. And it's Kaylie that brought me back.

HUGHIE. Kaylie.

BRIGIT. Coz I'd love to, ya know… have a normal life maybe… like you.

HUGHIE. Like me?!

BRIGIT. Well like people, other people, people who come into the caff and have their shoppin' and eat a scone and, ya know, live, just live, away from all the shite.

HUGHIE. Right.

BRIGIT. I'd like to live like that.

HUGHIE. Aye.

BRIGIT. That's my hope.

HUGHIE. Good.

BRIGIT. Yeah.

Pause.

Well have ya got that fixed?

HUGHIE. I have.

BRIGIT. Right. I'll have another go.

HUGHIE. Good woman…

Scene Six

BRIGIT *returns to the letter.*

BRIGIT. I don't know why I remember it all so clear Bernie… and it is – crystal, like no other time in me life. Maybe coz it was different, not different coz it wasn't Dublin, no. Different because I had that hope, I had something ahead.

HUGHIE *comes in, he sits like he is in the café.* BRIGIT *joins the memory. We hear the* RTÉ News *music overhead and the first few lines of the news.*

Here ya go Hughie.

That's me thanks for the paintin'!

HUGHIE. Ahh sure it was no bother Brigit.

BRIGIT. Ya did brilliant, ya did.

I got ya the extra eggs!

HUGHIE. Well isn't that mighty!

BRIGIT. Enjoy it now!

We vaguely hear the RTÉ News *now on a muffled voice-over as* HUGHIE *eats his dinner.*

VOICE-OVER. Digging is reported to have commenced at a bog near Navan County Meath for the body of a nineteen-year-old youth missing from Belfast since 1972. This is the third confirmed location of a body from the group now known as 'the disappeared'…

BRIGIT. Fuck… do ya hear that?

HUGHIE. Jesus.

BRIGIT. All the auld ones have been going on about it this morning.

Here's your tomato sauce.

HUGHIE. What?

BRIGIT. Your sauce.

HUGHIE. What?

BRIGIT. What's wrong with ya?

HUGHIE. What are they saying?

BRIGIT. Who?

HUGHIE. There… on the news.

BRIGIT. There was a murder. A body or something. A fella buried and they're digging in Oristown Bog.

HUGHIE. They're digging in Oristown bog?

BRIGIT. Yeah.

Is that our bog Hughie?

HUGHIE. Jesus.

BRIGIT. Is it?

HUGHIE. It is.

BRIGIT. So there's a body behind me house?!

HUGHIE. Shhhhh.

BRIGIT. Well that's fuckin' lovely that is.

HUGHIE. Please.

BRIGIT. I mean sweet dreams, Brigit, we hope ya sleep easy coz some poor fucker got a bullet in your garden…

HUGHIE. I need to hear it.

BRIGIT. Why?

HUGHIE. Who's digging?

BRIGIT. How should I know? The guards. The army. The police.

It's all on the news.

HUGHIE. And I can't hear it with your chirping.

BRIGIT. Charming!

HUGHIE. Please Brigit.

BRIGIT. And after me giving you extra eggs!

HUGHIE. I need to hear it.

BRIGIT. Why? Some fella was murdered… that's all they're saying! Some fella, years ago… by the IRA and now they're digging him up.

HUGHIE. But who's saying…?

BRIGIT. Your one! Someone! What's-her-face reads the news.

HUGHIE. So they're here.

BRIGIT. Looks like it. They're lookin' for information… the police… there's an amnesty or something… so they got a tip-off about the bog.

HUGHIE. An amnesty?

BRIGIT. Yeah.

HUGHIE. Someone's told them.

BRIGIT. Must have.

Jaysus what's wrong with ya Hughie?

HUGHIE. Nothing.

There's nothing wrong.

BRIGIT. Right.

Yeah.

Well… It doesn't make any sense… does it? Digging him up now… after what…

HUGHIE. Thirty years.

BRIGIT. Thirty years! Mother of Jesus… He's rotten! And what does he care? Whoever he is. Probably happy there… laying in that quiet… disappeared. Isn't he well away from the shite that brought the IRA to his door.

He looks at her.

What?

What's wrong with ya?

HUGHIE. I best get on.

BRIGIT. Ya best get on?

HUGHIE. I have to go.

BRIGIT. But what about your breakfast?

He is leaving.

Look I was only messin' Hughie… I was only messin' about the eggs!

Hughie!

HUGHIE. What?

BRIGIT. You won't forget me lift?

HUGHIE. What?

BRIGIT. Me lift… at two o'clock?!

HUGHIE. Oh, no.

No.

I won't forget.

BRIGIT. Only I've a load of shopping to get home.

HUGHIE. Sure thing.

BRIGIT. Okay? Okay, Hughie, I'll see you at two.

HUGHIE. Two.

BRIGIT. And here?!

HUGHIE. Two...

He is gone. She returns to her letter.

Scene Seven

BRIGIT. Now, that was a real shocker for me, Bernie... at the time like... hearing about Gerard's killing, his killing in my bog. I mean I know I wasn't even born when he was lifted... lifted from your house in Belfast, thirty year before... and in the dead of night I suppose. Jesus, I'm sorry about that. But it kind of took the gloss off Meath for me, ya know – hearing about it. Coz if killing could happen there, Bernie... Killin' and hidin' and lyin' in the peace of a place like that, well then I knew... I knew that there was really nowhere safe.

ANNIE *comes in, as if into* BRIGIT*'s house.*

Howaya Annie, come on in.

ANNIE. Hello Brigit, my goodness you have the place looking great!

BRIGIT Thanks!

And them police cars have nothing to do with me... I swear!

They both laugh.

ANNIE. I'm glad to hear it...

BRIGIT. They're with the diggers...they're diggin' for that boy.

From Northern Ireland...

ANNIE. Yes I read about it.

But I didn't realise it was so close... the site.

BRIGIT. Yeah.

ANNIE. Awful business.

BRIGIT. Yeah.

ANNIE. But look at you…

Keeping house!

BRIGIT. I am… amn't I?

ANNIE. When did you get it painted?

BRIGIT. At the weekend… I knew you were coming so I thought I'd surprise ya! Me friend helped…

ANNIE. Your friend?

BRIGIT. Well he's an auld fella really… a neighbour.

ANNIE. A neighbour?

BRIGIT. His name's Hughie – he's harmless, an auld fella like I said. But he taught me to ride a bike!

ANNIE. A bike?

BRIGIT. Yeah, me! Of all people! And I'm riding it into work…

ANNIE. Well that's fantastic, Brigit.

BRIGIT. Haven't missed a shift!

ANNIE. Yes. I heard!

BRIGIT. Progress!

ANNIE. Yes.

Definitely.

Progress!

BRIGIT. So you were talking to them in the job then?

ANNIE. I was…

BRIGIT. And they're happy with me?

ANNIE. They're very happy. You're doing great, Brigit.

BRIGIT. I'm doing great…!

Great!

ANNIE. Yes

BRIGIT. And I like it in the caff Annie. I never thought I'd say it… but I like it… and I like it here… in the bog, can you believe it?! I mean it's different… real different.

ANNIE. It is.

BRIGIT. And it seems kind of normal, do ya know? – Like what you'd see in books! I mean I know it's nothing excitin'… a caff! A house! But that's kind of exciting to me coz I've never known normal, have I Annie?

ANNIE. No.

BRIGIT. I've been out of me box since I can remember.

ANNIE. Yes.

BRIGIT. So sometimes I can't believe it's happenin'.

That I'm straight… and this is real.

ANNIE. It's real.

BRIGIT. Yeah!

ANNIE. But it's early days, Brigit.

BRIGIT. Oh yeah… it's early days.

ANNIE. And there's a way to go.

BRIGIT. Of course… of course… there's a way to go.

ANNIE. But I'm seeing progress.

BRIGIT. Good.

ANNIE. Real progress.

BRIGIT. Oh that's good, Annie.

Pause.

So have ya thought any more about the visit?

ANNIE. The visit?

BRIGIT. With Kaylie.

ANNIE. Oh yes. I have thought about it Brigit and I think, well maybe it is time... but it would have to be a supervised visit.

BRIGIT. Oh I know that... I know that, Jesus, anything, supervised Annie, whatever... just to see her... to see her. To see Kaylie that's all I want.

ANNIE. I'll see what I can do.

BRIGIT. Oh will ya? Please! It's been months... months but I'm together now, sure you can see it.

ANNIE. I can. I can see it Brigit.

BRIGIT. So you'll bring her... I mean it's over six months.

ANNIE. I'll try.

BRIGIT. Oh Jesus, if you bring her here... I could show her the garden... I could show her the birds... and make her dinner... a little dinner.

ANNIE. I'll put in a request.

BRIGIT. I do watch them in the caff, Annie, with the little babies... a bowl of mash... and I could make the gravy. I never made her nothing... but now I know how! Does she like gravy... can ya see if she likes gravy?

ANNIE. I'll ask.

BRIGIT. Oh thanks. Thanks, Annie. I won't let ya down. I promise. Here, sit down, have tea. I'll make ya tea. I've a pot and all... strawberries on it... it's not even nicked!

ANNIE. Well done!

BRIGIT. Jesus... you'll bring her here...

The memory fades out.

Scene Eight

BRIGIT *has entered* HUGHIE*'s house*.

HUGHIE. Who's that?

　　Who is it?

BRIGIT. It's me.

HUGHIE. What do ya want?

BRIGIT. Well that's charming, that is.

HUGHIE. Look what do ya want, Brigit? I'm busy.

BRIGIT. Oh yeah, it sure looks like it.

HUGHIE. I'm goin' out.

BRIGIT. Where?

HUGHIE. I'm just goin' out.

BRIGIT. Are ya now? And how about sorry for yesterday?!

HUGHIE. Hah?

BRIGIT. You stood me up!

HUGHIE. I what?

BRIGIT. You never collected me from the caff and me social
　　worker and all comin'!

HUGHIE. Oh. God.

BRIGIT. Yeah.

HUGHIE. I… I got caught.

BRIGIT. Where'd ya get caught?

HUGHIE. With Patsy Spillane, he had me trimming trees, I
　　forgot all about ya.

BRIGIT. Well cheers.

HUGHIE. Were ya all right?

BRIGIT. I hitched.

HUGHIE. Grand.

BRIGIT. No, it's not grand.

HUGHIE. Look I'm sorry.

BRIGIT. It's all right. I was worried about ya!

HUGHIE. About me?

BRIGIT. Yeah… What's goin' on with ya?

HUGHIE. Nothing. There's nothing going on.

BRIGIT. But you never forget stuff.

HUGHIE. I was trimming trees.

BRIGIT. Right.

HUGHIE. Yeah.

BRIGIT. Anyway – I've news!

HUGHIE. You've news?

BRIGIT. Yes! And it's about Kaylie.

HUGHIE. Kaylie?

BRIGIT. Yeah! She's comin' on a visit, Hughie.

HUGHIE. Is she?

BRIGIT. Yeah.

HUGHIE. The little one?

BRIGIT. Yeah.

HUGHIE. Imagine that.

BRIGIT. Oh, I'm fuckin' delighted, I am.

HUGHIE. You are, of course.

BRIGIT. I'll get to see her. I'll get to hold her. On Saturday.
Holy Jesus. Saturday. That's only three days away and she's
coming here.

HUGHIE. Here.

BRIGIT. To the house, yeah. So I need everything right.

HUGHIE. Oh, you do.

BRIGIT. Coz I need to prove meself, Hughie, prove that I'm doin' good.

HUGHIE. Aye.

BRIGIT. So I need you callin' in and all.

HUGHIE. Me?

BRIGIT. Yeah. On Saturday... Call like you're lookin' for a bit of help with somethin'... Like you're lookin' for sugar or that.

HUGHIE. Sugar?

BRIGIT. Yeah, sugar. Or anything that neighbours do be lookin' for. Jesus, Hughie, it's not a lot to ask!

HUGHIE. No, but...

BRIGIT. But what? I need to show them I'm coping, Hughie. That I'm movin' on, ya know. And it's important that Annie sees I've made friends.

HUGHIE. Friends.

BRIGIT. Well yeah. You're me friend.

HUGHIE *doesn't reply. She is uncomfortable.*

So you will call, won't ya?

HUGHIE. Oh, I will.

BRIGIT. Coz that's crucial. I need you, Hughie, and I need ya without all this nervous shite. The way you were, the way you usually are because this is me life, I mean Kaylie is everything, she is.

HUGHIE. Okay.

BRIGIT. Thanks.

HUGHIE. Grand.

BRIGIT. You'll call on Saturday?

HUGHIE. I will.

BRIGIT. And you won't forget.

HUGHIE. No, no.

She goes to leave.

Brigit!

BRIGIT. What?

HUGHIE. Would ya…

BRIGIT. What?

HUGHIE. Would ya do something for me then?

BRIGIT. Like what?

HUGHIE. Well something…

BRIGIT. Yeah…?

HUGHIE. Somethin', well you see, it's somethin'… serious.

BRIGIT. Serious?

HUGHIE. Yeah.

BRIGIT. And what do you mean by serious?

He pauses.

No. Do you know, it's all right. Don't tell me. Don't tell me coz I don't want to know. I've had me fair share of *serious*, Hughie. Serious beyond your wildest dreams so I don't care now if you've nicked someone's fucking turf or rode someone's wife or sheep or whatever coz I have me own stuff to be dealing with. Kaylie's comin' on a visit and it's not fair for you to be askin' me for anything.

HUGHIE. No.

BRIGIT. Now ya know it's not.

HUGHIE. No.

BRIGIT. I have to concentrate on me own stuff, yeah?

HUGHIE. Of course.

BRIGIT. So you just call in to me. Call in to me Saturday,
    Hughie, do the neighbourly bit, and head off, okay?

HUGHIE. Okay. No bother.

BRIGIT. Good. I'll see ya Saturday.

HUGHIE. Saturday, so.

She looks at him. She is unsettled. She leaves.

Scene Nine

BRIGIT *continues her letter.*

BRIGIT. I seen ya when you came to find him, Bernie. Find
    Gerard. I'm sure now it was you, surrounded by them
    bogmen guards, holding your flowers – and you see they all
    looked like they'd grown out of the brown, just squelched
    up out of it, hats and all. But you! No. You looked all wrong,
    with your tight white suit and sunglasses. Too stark against
    the slate grey of the sky and your red flowers for Gerard,
    blood red. You just seemed wrong.

    I had seen ya on me way home from Hughie's but it was
    later, much later when all the diggers had stopped and when
    the cars were gone that I went over. I went over to look at
    your flowers, to get a feel of your loss I suppose, coz I'm
    always attracted to shite, Bernie, and it was then I saw
    Gerard. Smilin' out at me he was from that photo you left.
    A big kid in a snorkle jacket – Polaroid colours... and the
    fluff of a moustache. That was Gerard, Gerard in Belfast I
    suppose, Gerard the lad. Gerard before he was disappeared.

I stood there ages, Bernie, just looking at your Gerard coz
there was something familiar in his eyes… I suppose I feel
disappeared meself, sometimes. No wonder they drove
Hughie mad.

BRIGIT *arrives home late at night.* HUGHIE *is waiting for
her. He gives her a fright.*

HUGHIE. Brigit.

BRIGIT. Wha'?

HUGHIE. I was waiting for ya.

BRIGIT. Jesus, Hughie, what are ya doing skulking around in
the dark?

HUGHIE. I was waitin' for ya.

BRIGIT. For wha'?

HUGHIE. I want to talk to ya.

BRIGIT. You want to talk to me?

You want to talk to me?

At ten o'clock at night you want to talk to me?

HUGHIE. Brigit…

BRIGIT. Jesus, suddenly everyone wants to talk!

The bleedin' manager kept me till this hour coz she wanted
to talk! She's changin' her bleedin menus: Chicken à la King.
As if I give a fuck…! I mean Kaylie's comin' tomorrow and
I'm stood there talking fuckin' mushrooms…

HUGHIE. Can I come in, Brigit?

BRIGIT. No, ya can't come in, Hughie.

Ya can't come in, coz I've got to do stuff, can't ya see I've
got to do stuff?

HUGHIE. But.

BRIGIT. Will ya move!

You're in the way of me bike.

HUGHIE. Oh... I'm sorry.

BRIGIT. Fuckin' ten o'clock!

I've to clean the house and all, I do.

HUGHIE. But, Brigit.

BRIGIT. What?

HUGHIE. Please...! Please!

BRIGIT. Please what?

Jesus, would ya get a grip of yourself?

You're startin' to give me the creeps.

HUGHIE. I'm sorry, I'm so sorry.

BRIGIT. And what's that in your hand?

HUGHIE. Hah?

BRIGIT. What's that in your hand, Hughie?

HUGHIE. Oh... it's... it's a photo.

BRIGIT. A photo?

HUGHIE. It was out on the bog.

BRIGIT. Out on the bog?

HUGHIE. And I found it.

BRIGIT. Ya did?

HUGHIE. Yeah... I did.

BRIGIT. Right.

HUGHIE. So I want... I need...

BRIGIT. Yeah.

Yeah, yeah... I hear ya.

I hear ya, Hughie, so I'll tell ya what. Me and you... after... after Kaylie... after me visit, we'll talk. We'll talk about everything... we'll talk till the bleedin' cows come home... okay?

HUGHIE. Will we, Brigit?

BRIGIT. Yeah... but just... just give me me afternoon, yeah? I don't need all this unravelling, Hughie... I just don't need any hassle... coz... well... please?

Pause.

HUGHIE. Right.

BRIGIT. Yeah.

HUGHIE. I'll call tomorrow.

BRIGIT. Just like we said?

HUGHIE. Aye.

BRIGIT. Like we planned it.

HUGHIE. Aye.

BRIGIT. Thanks.

HUGHIE. Okay.

And I'm sorry Brigit...

I'm sorry...

He is gone.

Scene Ten

DARREN, BRIGIT*'s ex, arrives at the house with a babyseat. He stands in shite.*

DARREN. Fucksake.

BRIGIT. Darren!

DARREN. Me new runners and I just stood in shite!

BRIGIT. Ooh look, look at her, Kaylie.

It's your mammy.

DARREN. Take it easy she's sleepin'.

BRIGIT. Oh right. Yeah. Sorry. Come on in, where's Annie?

DARREN. Would ya look at me runners.

BRIGIT. Sure I'll clean them, it's just muck. Ya get used to it.

DARREN. Jaysus. Kip.

They are inside BRIGIT*'s house now.*

BRIGIT. Right.

DARREN. Yeah.

BRIGIT. Do ya want to sit down?

DARREN. Right.

BRIGIT. Here.

DARREN. Right.

BRIGIT. So.

DARREN. Yeah.

BRIGIT. How are ya?

DARREN. Grand.

BRIGIT. Yeah.

DARREN. Yeah... and you?

BRIGIT. Great.

DARREN. Great.

BRIGIT. Sticking to everything.

DARREN. Oh yeah?

BRIGIT. Yeah.

Can I just have a look at her?

DARREN. She's sleepin'.

BRIGIT. I know, I won't disturb her... Oh Jesus... look... Oh,
Darren, would ya look at her?

DARREN. I'm always lookin' at her.

BRIGIT. Oh my God, the size of her… I can't believe it.

Hello… hello little girl… hello… it's your mama… it's your mama.

DARREN. You'll wake her, Jaysus where's your one, all her stuff is in the car.

BRIGIT. Will I put her in me room… I've the heater on.

DARREN. She's grand.

BRIGIT. And a real soft blankey… I got in Tesco… I'll bring her in.

DARREN. She's grand, I said.

BRIGIT. Okay, okay Darren.

DARREN. We're not stayin' long.

BRIGIT. Oh.

DARREN. Where the hell is this anyway.

BRIGIT. It's not far from Navan.

DARREN. It's the middle of bleedin' nowhere is where it is.

Jaysus where is that bitch?

ANNIE. Sorry guys. I got a call. My God, what have you got in this bag Darren, it weighs a tonne.

DARREN. I dunno, me ma packed it.

ANNIE. Right, well, here we are Brigit.

BRIGIT. Yeah. Yeah. Thanks Annie! Will yiz have lunch?

ANNIE. Lunch! Lovely.

BRIGIT. I made soup!

ANNIE. Soup…! Well done Brigit.

BRIGIT. Carrot.

ANNIE. Well isn't that marvellous? Will you have some Darren?

DARREN. No.

ANNIE. Okay.

BRIGIT. Or a ham sandwich... I made a ham sandwich?

ANNIE. Ham sandwich?

DARREN. No.

BRIGIT. Are ya sure, I took the crusts off.

DARREN. Go on then.

BRIGIT. Great... there in the kitchen.

ANNIE. Well I'll get them... you stay here with Kaylie, Brigit.

BRIGIT. Can I...? Thanks.

ANNIE exits.

Oh my God... she's gettin' big, Darren.

DARREN. Yeah.

BRIGIT. And ya have her gorgeous... fair play to ya... the little shoes!

DARREN. That's me ma, she dotes over her she does...

BRIGIT. Right.

Hello little girl, your mammy's here, yeah... yeahhh...

DARREN. Look leave her sleep, why don't ya?

BRIGIT. But I never see her.

DARREN. Yeah, well whose fault is that?

BRIGIT. Ahh fuck off Darren.

DARREN. Right I'll fuck off and bring her with me and where'll that leave ya?

We hear the sound of the baby crying.

BRIGIT. No no please.

DARREN. Look ya have her fuckin' cryin' now.

BRIGIT. No please I'm sorry… here Kaylie, here Kaylie… Mammy's here.

DARREN. You're not fit to have her near ya.

BRIGIT. I'm sorry… please… here, Kaylie, don't cry.

DARREN. I knew this was a stupid idea…

Will ya lift her out of the bleedin'…

BRIGIT. I can't… the belt is…

DARREN. Fucksake.

BRIGIT. Here, she's all right. She's probably hungry. I'll give her her dinner.

DARREN. There's a bottle in the bag.

BRIGIT. I made her her dinner.

DARREN. Give her the fuckin' bottle…

BRIGIT. Okay… okay… Thanks, Darren. I have it. I have it now.

DARREN. Yeah yeah. I'm goin' out for a smoke.

BRIGIT. Out?

DARREN. I don't smoke round Kaylie.

BRIGIT. Oh.

BRIGIT *gives the baby her bottle*.

Ahh here ya are… here ya are, baba… it's all right… did we wake ya… did we… bold Mammy… poor Kaylie…

DARREN. And don't get too comfortable coz me ma wants us back before six.

BRIGIT. You only just got here.

DARREN. Kaylie has her routine!

BRIGIT. All right, Jesus.

　　All right.

DARREN. And remember, Brigit, I know ya. Ya might have this clueless cunt codded but I seen ya fuck it up... every time.

BRIGIT. Not this time, Darren, I'm clean!

DARREN. Yeah, yeah.

　　DARREN *exits*.

　　ANNIE *is back with sandwiches*.

BRIGIT. Look at her guzzling, Annie.

ANNIE. Her mammy knew she was hungry!

BRIGIT. Oh God. I can't believe I'm holding her. It's like a dream it is.

ANNIE. She's lovely.

BRIGIT. She's beautiful. Aren't ya... aren't ya beautiful?

　　Thanks for swingin' this Annie... I can't... I don't know...

ANNIE. You've earned it.

BRIGIT. Yeah. Jaysus... look at her... halfway through the bottle.

　　They dote and coo.

ANNIE. You're a natural, Brigit.

BRIGIT. Thanks.

ANNIE. And she is doing so well.

BRIGIT. Is she?

ANNIE. She's hit all her targets.

BRIGIT. Clever girl.

ANNIE. It's good she's with Darren... Brigit. Keep her with family. His mother is a great support.

BRIGIT. Yeah… ya mean he does fuck-all. Sure it's all they ever wanted anyway… to get me outta the picture…

ANNIE. Well. You didn't help yourself…

BRIGIT. I know… don't ya think I know that now, Annie!

DARREN. Hey Brigit there's some auld fella out here lookin' for ya.

BRIGIT. Wha'?

DARREN. Some looney by the looks of him.

BRIGIT. Who is it…? Oh it must be Hughie. He's the neighbour, Annie.

ANNIE. Oh yes the neighbour!

BRIGIT. I do give him a bit of chat now and again… he's lonely, ya know.

ANNIE. Oh right, well it will be great to meet him.

BRIGIT. And it's very non-threatenin' like ya know, Annie, the relationship, out of me usual cycle altogether… he's an auld fella.

ANNIE. Right.

BRIGIT. Jaysus it is Hughie!

Gas, come on in!

HUGHIE. Sugar!

BRIGIT. Great.

HUGHIE. So. How are ya?

BRIGIT. Great. I'm great, I'm delighted ya called Hughie coz Kaylie's here she is.

HUGHIE. Ahh the little one.

BRIGIT. Yeah.

HUGHIE. Lovely.

BRIGIT. Would ya let him in, Darren! He's me friend... Hughie.

HUGHIE. Sure, I can come back later if it's...

BRIGIT. No come on in... come on, I was just tellin' Annie about ya.

ANNIE. Hello.

BRIGIT. This is Annie and this is Kaylie... they brought her down they did...

HUGHIE. Ahh, Brigit.

BRIGIT. Yeah. I'm thrilled... would ya come on in, for God's sake... we're havin' tea.

HUGHIE. Well sure...

BRIGIT. This is Hughie.

ANNIE. Great to meet you.

HUGHIE. Oh aye.

I just live over the road.

BRIGIT. And that's Darren, Kaylie's da.

HUGHIE. Hello.

DARREN. Yeah.

BRIGIT. Don't mind him.

Will you have a cup of tea, Hughie, or a sandwich?

HUGHIE. Ahh no I won't stay.

DARREN. So what did ya call for?

BRIGIT. Jesus, Darren.

DARREN. What?

BRIGIT. Don't mind him. Sit down, Hughie, come on, here's me princess.

HUGHIE. Ahh Jesus.

BRIGIT. Upsa-daisy... say hello to Uncle Hughie.

DARREN. You'll make her puke bouncing her like that.

BRIGIT. I won't, Darren.

ANNIE. Brigit says you've become good friends.

HUGHIE. Ahh sure.

BRIGIT. He's dead interested in me paintin' aren't ya Hughie...
Here do ya want to hold her?

DARREN. For fucksake, Brigit.

BRIGIT. What?

ANNIE. You might just calm down there, Darren.

DARREN. You're not passin' me daughter to that!

HUGHIE. Look sure it's all right.

The baby starts crying.

DARREN. Stay away from her right.

HUGHIE. Look now, I don't want to cause any trouble.

BRIGIT. There's no trouble, Hughie... Darren's just bein' a
prick.

ANNIE. Stop it now guys.

HUGHIE. Maybe I better be off...

BRIGIT. No, Hughie...! I want you here.

She tries to jostle him and HUGHIE *falls over a chair.*

Jesus.

HUGHIE. I'm all right.

DARREN. Oh this is fuckin' beautiful, this is.

BRIGIT. Fuck off you.

ANNIE. Are you all right?

HUGHIE. I'm grand.

DARREN. Class.

ANNIE. That's enough, Darren.

HUGHIE. I wasn't... I'm sorry.

ANNIE. It's fine, really... did you hurt yourself?

Baby ups the crying.

HUGHIE. I'm sorry now I shouldn't have called.

BRIGIT. No no, it wasn't your fault.

DARREN. Bleedin' pisshead.

BRIGIT. He's not.

ANNIE. I think that's enough now, Darren.

HUGHIE. I'm sorry, I just... I must have just...

DARREN. Fell fuckin' over.

HUGHIE. I'll just be goin'.

BRIGIT. No!

ANNIE. I'll help you out.

HUGHIE leaves with ANNIE.

DARREN. Fuckin' typical.

BRIGIT. Just give her back to me, will ya, she's all upset.

DARREN. Bleedin' right... would ya look at the mother she has.

BRIGIT. Please, Darren.

DARREN. Money must be good if you're shaggin' that.

BRIGIT. He's just me friend.

DARREN. He is yeah. Look I'm outta here I am and so's Kaylie... nothin's changed...

BRIGIT. No Darren, he's me neighbour.

DARREN. All over the shop he was and you were goin' to drop me daughter in his lap.

BRIGIT. She's MY daughter.

DARREN. Not since you tried to fuck her in the canal she isn't.

BRIGIT. Don't.

DARREN. Don't what? Do ya think I forget that Brigit? Do you think you can just make a fuckin' sandwich and wipe it away?

BRIGIT. Please.

DARREN. Off your face as always Brigit, weren't you, and dangling her... dangling Kaylie... like she was a rat!

BRIGIT. No!

DARREN. So don't be foolin' yourself... you'll never be her mammy coz you're not fit.

BRIGIT. I am. I am her mammy.

DARREN. Ya see I'm only humourin' these assholes. Humouring them, Brigit, like me ma said, till you fuck it up so bad the social won't let ya near her either.

BRIGIT. No ya can't.

She goes to hit him just as ANNIE *returns.*

ANNIE. Brigit. Christ!

DARREN. Now! Do you see what you're dealing with!

BRIGIT. I want Kaylie, I want her back... I want me life back Darren.

ANNIE. Calm down Brigit.

DARREN. The only life you get is the one that I give ya.

ANNIE. Come on, that's enough.

DARREN. And don't you forget it.

DARREN *is gone.*

BRIGIT. No, give her back, give me my baby back... don't let him, Annie, don't let him.

ANNIE. I'm sorry… we'll have to go.

BRIGIT. No!

ANNIE. You need to calm down. Look we'll talk about this.

We'll talk about it.

DARREN. Are you fuckin' comin' or what?

They exit.

BRIGIT. No… please

Please… I want Kaylie. I want Kaylie, Annie…

I'm different now. I wouldn't hurt her. Please. She wants her mammy, please, she wants her mammy, Kaylie… please.

She is left alone and sobbing.

Scene Eleven

BRIGIT *picks herself up and goes back to where she writes her letter.*

BRIGIT. I've always known where Gerard lies, Bernie. Hughie told me when I was there, when the guards were digging, when ya brought them flowers to the bog. He wanted me to help, he wanted to tell because the silence had driven him crazy and the guilt had never left.

BRIGIT *returns to her memory. She has called to* HUGHIE's *house.*

HUGHIE *is in tatters. He turns and walks back into the house.* BRIGIT *follows.*

You drinkin'?

HUGHIE. I am.

BRIGIT. Any cans?

HUGHIE. No, just that.

BRIGIT. I hate whiskey.

HUGHIE. There's tea.

BRIGIT. Fuck it.

She takes the bottle.

I'm sorry about today.

HUGHIE. Sure Jesus it's me who is sorry.

BRIGIT. No... a disaster it was.

HUGHIE. I just didn't see, I didn't see the chair...!

BRIGIT. It wasn't your fault.

HUGHIE. No?

BRIGIT. Fuckin' nothing new in it.

HUGHIE. No?

BRIGIT. Everything I touch turns to disaster Hughie... even here.

HUGHIE. I'm sorry.

BRIGIT. Are ya all right? Did you hurt yourself?

HUGHIE. No. No. I didn't hurt myself. I'm grand.

BRIGIT. Well you don't look grand.

HUGHIE. No.

BRIGIT. No.

Pause.

Why were ya pissed Hughie?

HUGHIE. I'm sorry.

BRIGIT. And last night!

I mean I've never seen ya pissed.

HUGHIE. No.

BRIGIT. Oh, fuck it.

She drinks. Pause.

HUGHIE. I seen his face, Brigit.

BRIGIT. Whose face?

HUGHIE. The boy in the bog.

BRIGIT. What's it to do with you, Hughie… what's it to do with you?

HUGHIE. The photo.

BRIGIT. I know. I put it back.

It's back with the flowers.

HUGHIE. They're the same eyes… the same face.

BRIGIT. Same as what?

HUGHIE. Jesus Christ, help me.

BRIGIT. What?

HUGHIE. Will ya help me, Brigit?

BRIGIT. But help ya what?

HUGHIE. The boy.

BRIGIT. Yeah?

HUGHIE. He…

BRIGIT. He what?

HUGHIE. Oh, I'm nearly gone mad from it.

BRIGIT. But from what?

HUGHIE. He…

BRIGIT. Tell me… will ya. Just fuckin' tell me.

He sighs.

There is a flashback to the night of Gerard's murder. We see young HUGHIE *and his friend* CONOR. *This can be done cinematically or played, again it is up to the directorial style. It should be muffled and vague, criss-crossed with images of lights and eyes – muddled like a traumatic memory.*

HUGHIE. It's feckin' freezin' down here.

CONOR. Don't I know it is, Hughie.

HUGHIE. Give us another one of them cans so.

CONOR. I will in me arse... ya gave me no money for them.

HUGHIE. Didn't I come with ya.

CONOR. And why wouldn't ya do your bit.

HUGHIE. Ahh, go on Conor, just one... I'll give ya a fag.

CONOR. Go on then.

HUGHIE. Good man.

Shudders.

Jaysus, is that a car?

CONOR. Sounds like it, all right.

HUGHIE. Is it them?

CONOR. How would I feckin' know...

HUGHIE. How many guns are they bringin'?

CONOR. I dunno.

HUGHIE. Where'd they get them?

CONOR. I dunno, Hughie... for fuck's sake. Seamie just told me to meet him here and bring a shovel...

HUGHIE. That car's at the cross in the bog now.

CONOR. Well get the torch out.

HUGHIE. Shh, it's stoppin' now.

BRIGIT *interrupts the memory.*

BRIGIT. You were there?

HUGHIE. I was Brigit.

BRIGIT. What the fuck?

HUGHIE. I thought it was guns, I swear it. I thought it was guns we were burying. I never dreamt it could be a boy...

BRIGIT. He was dead?

HUGHIE. No… no.

BRIGIT. Jesus, ya shot him?

HUGHIE. No!

> There were four of them in the car, Brigit. And me and Conor with the hole dug. Jes, we thought we were the real men, the big men, till we saw what they pulled from the boot. His face was torn from punching and the waif-like twist of a body like death against the bog.

BRIGIT. Jesus.

HUGHIE. He hadn't a screed on him, Brigit, I don't know if they stripped him or had just pulled him from the bed.

> Who's this, says I? 'A rat,' says one of them, 'and this is what we do to a rat.'

There is a loud gunshot.

> 'You take a good look at that now, son, and remember to keep your gob shut.'

> And he fell, the boy, he just fell like broken snow into the hole I dug an hour before… but not before he locked eyes on me – somewhere between the 'who' and the shot, he caught me in those eyes – and the fear was gone from them now. Just shock. Shock that this was his end, this was his miserable finish.

BRIGIT. Jesus.

HUGHIE. He was no older than meself at the time.

BRIGIT. What did ya do?

HUGHIE. Sure what could I do?

> Nothin'.

BRIGIT. Nothing?

HUGHIE. I was terrified.

BRIGIT. But what about your mate?

HUGHIE. Conor… he left for the States. I never heard from him after…

BRIGIT. And they never came back?

HUGHIE. No. Never. I was afraid they would for a long time but the world, the war… it moved on.

BRIGIT. Fuckin' hell.

HUGHIE. But now I think we have a chance, Brigit.

BRIGIT. What?

HUGHIE. I think we have a chance to make amends.

BRIGIT. What?

HUGHIE. Because I want them to know.

BRIGIT. Who to know?

HUGHIE. The police… the guards.

BRIGIT. The guards? Know now? Are ya mad?

HUGHIE. You see I need them to know.

BRIGIT. Why?

HUGHIE. So I can have some peace.

BRIGIT. But you'll be arrested.

HUGHIE. I don't care any more, Brigit, I need to tell them because they're digging in the wrong place.

BRIGIT. They're what?

HUGHIE. They'll not find him that side of the bog.

BRIGIT. This is fuckin' nuts.

HUGHIE. So will you tell them for me, Brigit.

BRIGIT. Me!

HUGHIE. Yes, you see, I can't. I've tried all week but I can't. I've not had the courage for thirty years Brigit and I don't have it now.

BRIGIT. And you expect me to do it?

HUGHIE. Please. Please Brigit. If you tell them, they can take the boy home.

BRIGIT. No.

HUGHIE. Take him home where he belongs.

BRIGIT. No, I said.

HUGHIE. He's at Cannonstown Cross.

BRIGIT. Would ya fuck off?

HUGHIE. Face-down in the dirt Brigit. Face-down...

BRIGIT. No... no way, Hughie. You can just leave me out of this.

HUGHIE. But...

BRIGIT. But nothin' Hughie... this isn't right... this isn't part of the deal...

HUGHIE. But there's an amnesty, Brigit, there'll be no trouble.

BRIGIT. But this is your trouble, Hughie. It has nothin' to do with me. I got me own stuff, for Christ's sake... haven't I enough to be dealin' with?

HUGHIE. Brigit!

BRIGIT. And I thought you were different... I thought you were... for once... just for once... someone... someone good... someone decent. Someone who didn't want shit from me... but you're just as bad.... no, you're worse... worse than Darren, worse than me da... worse than any of them... usin' me.

HUGHIE. Brigit.

BRIGIT. Using me to do your dirt.

HUGHIE. No please.

BRIGIT. So you can rot, Hughie Dolan. You can rot, just like that poor bastard in the bog.

She exits. HUGHIE *is crushed.*

Fade.

Scene Twelve

BRIGIT *resumes her letter.*

BRIGIT. Hughie's dead now, Bernie. I just heard that today. Ya see I left Meath. Left Meath that night and no surprises there. Took a bus back to Dublin and all that came with it. Went back on the smack. And back on the game. Like Darren said I would.

But I saw him once after, Hughie. I was in Navan with a bloke on a deal... and I got him to drive out... out to my bog. Jaysus, ya should have seen the house... Hughie's house... it was wrecked, it was... gate hangin'... no paint on the door... you'd think there was no one livin' in it. But I saw him... I saw him through the winda... and the smell... you could get it from outside... and he was just sittin' there, sittin' in a chair... bottle in hand... eyes on the floor.

I never even went inside.

And I never got Kaylie, Bernie... never got nothing. I disappeared.

You'll find Gerard at Cannonstown Cross. Face-down, Hughie said face-down Bernie and still waiting to go home.

The End.

WILD NOTES

Wild Notes was first performed in 2018 as part of The Frederick Douglass Project by Solas Nua in Washington, DC. The cast was as follows:

Gary Perkins III
Madeline Mooney
Daniel Westbrook
Louis Davis
Jenny Donovan
Tiffany Byrd
Kevin Collins
Michael Crowley

Director	Raymond O. Caldwell
Choreography	Tiffany Quinn
Scenic Design	Jonathan Dahm Roberston
Lighting Design	Marianne Meadows
Costume Design	Danielle Preston
Music Director	Michael Winch
Dramaturg/Dialect Coach	Rex Daugherty
Artistic Director	Rex Daugherty

Characters

MARGARET KEANE, *nineteen, white Irish*
FREDERICK DOUGLASS, *twenty-seven, Black American*
KABITE, *a young Ugandan woman*
RITA, *a young Dublin woman who looks twenty-six but
    functioning at the mental age of seven*
KALIEF, *a young black man in a prisoner's uniform*

A woman stands on the quayside, singing. She is MARGARET
KEANE, *nineteen and dressed in clothes of the period – 1845.
She is singing 'The Croppy Boy' (an old Irish rebel song).*
FREDERICK DOUGLASS *is walking along the quayside. He
is caught by her singing. When she finishes her song he throws a
coin into her cup.*

DOUGLASS. Thank you.

> *She doesn't reply.*

> May I enquire as to the nature of your song?

MARGARET. Didn't you hear it?

> Or why did you throw me your guinea?

DOUGLASS. Pardon me, perhaps I should alter my question.

> I am curious to know what is a croppy boy?

MARGARET. A croppy boy?

> A croppy boy is a rebel, sir.

DOUGLASS. A rebel?

MARGARET. Yes.

DOUGLASS. What class of a rebel?

MARGARET. The class that wants freedom, sir.

DOUGLASS. Freedom?

MARGARET. Of course.

DOUGLASS. Freedom from what?

> MARGARET *laughs.*

MARGARET. Where is it that you are from, sir?

DOUGLASS. Why do you ask?

MARGARET. Because it is clear that you know nothing of
Ireland.

DOUGLASS. Indeed. Indeed. I know very little of Ireland as I
am only recently arrived.

MARGARET. I see.

DOUGLASS. Please tell me about this croppy boy?

MARGARET. Why?

DOUGLASS. Or is there a croppy girl perhaps?

MARGARET. I'm sure there was an army of croppy girls but
who would bother to take up a tune in their name?

DOUGLASS. Would you not take up the pen yourself to tell
their story?

MARGARET. I am afraid I'm a little too occupied with staying
alive, sir.

DOUGLASS. Staying alive?

Are conditions really so bad here?

MARGARET. Haven't you two eyes in your head?

Look around this quay and tell me what you see?

DOUGLASS. I see... I admit I see great wretchedness here.

MARGARET. Indeed you do.

DOUGLASS. But I confess I do not understand it.

MARGARET. Oh it's a puzzle all right, sir.

It's a puzzle to see Irish men, women and children roam
here amidst the debris and filth, half-starved and about to
be evicted from their own country. It is a puzzle to see them
board ships not fit for a dog at the behest of their government
and landlords. It is a puzzle to see their eyes wild with want
and their lips green from sucking grass. It is a puzzle to see
their bellies swollen from famine when these ships that stand
along the quay are bursting with Irish grain, bursting with

Irish wheat and Irish horses, seed and cattle. But these ships are bound for Liverpool, sir, and their bounty is bound for the English gut. The Irish... the Irish are left to die here along the quay, or in their fields.

DOUGLASS. But why?

MARGARET. Because Ireland is but a colony, sir. Ireland serves her English master. Don't you know that? Don't you know that those men you walked with earlier support an English monarch and care nothing for us, nothing for me?

DOUGLASS. You saw me earlier?

MARGARET. I did. And I saw the English masters that you walked with. The same masters that killed my croppy boy and abandon the likes of me to the coffin ships.

DOUGLASS. Coffin ships, why do you call them coffin ships?

MARGARET. Because most of us die in them, sir, packed ten to a dozen in the cattle hold. Most of us never reach the New World but find our future with the fishes in the forgotten depths of the ocean.

DOUGLASS. But this is terrible... if it is true?

MARGARET. Why would you doubt me, sir?

DOUGLASS. Why indeed?

May I ask you your name?

MARGARET. You may.

DOUGLASS. What is your name?

MARGARET. My name is Margaret, sir. Margaret Keane.

DOUGLASS. It is a pleasure to be acquainted with you, Margaret Keane.

MARGARET. And what is yours?

DOUGLASS. My name is Frederick Douglass.

MARGARET. May God bless you, Frederick Douglass.

DOUGLASS. You appear to be educated, despite your poor condition.

MARGARET. Is that such a surprise?

DOUGLASS. No, no, please do not misunderstand me.

I know what it is to be judged by appearance, to be presumed ignorant, incapable of philosophy or thought.

MARGARET. Do you?

DOUGLASS. I do.

MARGARET. Well it doesn't take a philosopher to see wretchedness, sir, nor to understand the greed behind it.

DOUGLASS. Greed?

MARGARET. Greed is the only explanation for what England does to me and mine.

Pause.

DOUGLASS. But how then are you educated?

MARGARET. Because my father was a schoolteacher.

DOUGLASS. Is that so?

MARGARET. It is. And his classroom was a ditch because England doesn't want the likes of me to be book-reading and England doesn't want the likes of me to understand her politics or her greed.

DOUGLASS. I was a teacher myself once.

MARGARET. Were you?

DOUGLASS. Yes. Sunday school. I taught Sunday school in Maryland, also from a ditch. Yet I believe they were the happiest days of my life.

MARGARET. And what are you now, sir, if not a teacher?

DOUGLASS. What am I now?

MARGARET. Yes.

DOUGLASS. I am.

    I am a writer.

    I am a speaker.

    I speak here in Ireland...

MARGARET. Speak?

DOUGLASS. Yes.

MARGARET. Well that's a grand job altogether.

    What is it that you speak of?

DOUGLASS. My life.

    My life in slavery.

MARGARET. Slavery?

DOUGLASS. Yes.

MARGARET. But where is it that you are from, sir?

DOUGLASS. I am from the United States of America.

MARGARET. America?

DOUGLASS. Yes.

MARGARET. But that's where I'm going.

DOUGLASS. It seems to me that that is where every wretch here is going.

MARGARET. Well of course it is. Sure isn't it only in America that you will find a gentleman the likes of yourself. A gentleman that is as black as the night. They say that America is a place where anything can happen, where anyone can find sanctuary or hope.

DOUGLASS. Who says that?

MARGARET. Every wretch.

DOUGLASS. Now I am the one who is afraid that you know nothing of America.

MARGARET. Why do you say that?

How can you say that, sir?

When America…

America is the dream.

KABITE, *a young Ugandan woman in contemporary dress, appears.*

KABITE. Where do I find sanctuary?

Tell me, where do I find hope?

If not in America?

My sister and I were sleeping soundly in our bed, dreaming children's dreams, when the Lord's Resistance Army came into our village. We were ten years old, when the Lord's soldiers broke down the door and tore us out into the black night. The soldiers dragged us, kicking and screaming over the broken body of our mother and told us to march in a line with our neighbours out into the bush, and far from home. If we resisted, they told us they would kill us.

I was forced to hold a gun and learn how to shoot it.

I was forced to lie with a brigade commander as his wife.

I was forced to beat my twin sister and to hold a gun to her head when she displeased her husband.

My sister was a like a broken doll when last I saw her; bleeding, crying, shivering, lost.

The first time I was raped by my new husband I too tried to fight back.

But such husbands have guns.

Such husbands kill without conscience.

And such husbands beat their young wives to within an inch of their lives.

I learnt how to hold a gun.

I learnt how to kill without mercy.

I learnt how to keep my husband's other wives in line when he was away because if one of them escaped, I would be killed.

I learnt how to do unspeakable things as a slave in the Lord's Army.

It was the only way to survive.

Two years into my captivity our unit came into battle with government soldiers.

I used this as an opportunity to escape.

I ran from the Lord's Army.

I dropped my gun and told my story.

The government soldiers treated me with kindness.

Kindness!

It made me cry.

I cried for hours.

I cried for days.

I cried for every bullet that I had fired.

I cried for every time I was forced to open my legs.

I cried for every face that I saw murdered.

I cried for those that I had murdered myself.

I cried for my sister.

I cried for me.

The soldiers gave me food and clothes and took me home to my village.

But my village is a different place now and I am a very different girl.

My mother did not survive her beating.

My father cannot forgive me my past.

I am haunted by the loss of my sister.

I am terrified that I will be found.

By my husband.

By his army.

I cannot stay in Uganda.

I cannot stay in Sudan.

So where do I go now?

What new world will open up her heart to me?

Or am I forever to be…

Refugee?

MARGARET *starts to sing 'The Last Rose of Summer' by Thomas Moore.*

KABITE *joins her, but neither* DOUGLASS *nor* MARGARET *acknowledge her presence.*

DOUGLASS. That is another beautiful song, Margaret.

MARGARET. You will find that we are full of beautiful songs here.

DOUGLASS. But songs don't make you free.

MARGARET. No. Songs don't make you free, sir.

I will be free when I find work as a teacher in America.

DOUGLASS. Is that so?

MARGARET. I hope so. They say that they have women teachers in America.

DOUGLASS. I believe they do.

MARGARET. Good.

She smiles.

DOUGLASS. Your singing reminds me of the wild notes of the cotton field.

MARGARET. I'm not sure that I understand you, sir.

DOUGLASS. Why do you sing, Margaret?

MARGARET. Why do I sing?

DOUGLASS. Yes.

MARGARET. I sing because I have to.

I sing to remember... sometimes.

I sing to forget... sometimes.

I sing to dream.

DOUGLASS. To dream?

MARGARET. Yes.

DOUGLASS. And what is it that you dream of?

MARGARET. I dream of love.

I dream of hope.

I dream of a home.

DOUGLASS. I also dream of a home.

MARGARET. Surely you have one, sir, with your tweed suit and strong boots and silk shirt?

DOUGLASS. I thought we agreed not to judge each other by our appearances?

MARGARET. I have agreed to nothing...

DOUGLASS. I dream of freedom too, Margaret.

I have been dreaming of freedom since I was a boy.

A boy that stood as you do now, at the edge of a great water, at the edge of a great abyss, but I am not permitted to dream.

I am not permitted to dream of any other condition for the black man.

Any other state, or law.

Because I am told that it is God's will that I be a slave.

That I live in slavery.

Die in slavery.

But something in me, Margaret, something in me, Margaret Keane, tells me that freedom is out there.

Somewhere.

Upstream.

Upriver.

Not far.

MARGARET. And why do you tell me all this, sir?

DOUGLASS. Perhaps because of your song.

Because of your croppy boy.

MARGARET. I'm afraid my croppy boy was hanged, sir.

My croppy boy was tortured. Betrayed. Denied.

DOUGLASS. Yet he lives on, Margaret.

He lives on in your song!

MARGARET (*smiles*). I suppose he does.

DOUGLASS. To dream is a powerful thing.

MARGARET. I hope so.

He goes to walk away.

Does that mean that you found it?

DOUGLASS. Found what?

MARGARET. Your freedom, sir?

DOUGLASS. Almost.

MARGARET. Almost?

DOUGLASS. I think I find it here, Margaret Keane.

I think I find moments of it here.

MARGARET. In Ireland?

DOUGLASS. Yes. In Ireland there are moments when I am treated as a man.

When I encounter none of the prejudice of America.

MARGARET. But what is this prejudice that you speak of?

I have heard nothing of it.

DOUGLASS. In America, I am slave.

In America, I am chattel that can be bought or sold.

In America, I can be flogged or starved or murdered with no law to protect me.

In America, I am less than a man.

MARGARET. Less than a woman?

DOUGLASS. Less than a free woman.

MARGARET. I won't. I don't believe you, sir.

DOUGLASS. But what I say is true.

MARGARET. But on what account?

DOUGLASS. On account of the colour of my skin.

How did you describe it?

'As black as the night.'

MARGARET *reaches out her hand to touch his face.*

MARGARET. But the night can be comforting, sir.

And the night can be where you find truth.

The night can be beautiful, sir.

And can shield you in her cloak.

RITA, *a young Dublin woman who looks twenty-six but functioning at the mental age of seven, appears.*

RITA. Me and my granny always loved the night.

The day's work over.

The dinner ate.

Fire lit.

Telly on.

And we would have our smoke.

My granny loved her smoke.

I'd only be let have the one smoke with her because she said that they were bad for me.

John Player Blue.

And a BIC lighter.

Balanced on her armchair.

And fingernails always painted pink.

I loved my granny from the day I was born.

I loved her rusty voice.

I loved her shepherd's pie.

I loved her smell of face powder and Oil of Ulay.

I loved the way she dried my hair and sat me in front of the fire.

My granny didn't mind that I was touched by God.

My granny didn't make me go to the special school.

My granny kept me at home.

She said that I was her comfort in life now that there was just the two of us.

Now that mammy had died from the heroin, I was her little pal, her girl.

My granny worked as a cleaner on Thomas Street.

She cleaned at the art school.

She loved to get her hair done on a Friday and she would bring me to Gaye's Hairdressers.

And I would get a wash and blow-dry and Gaye didn't mind that I was touched either. She loved me she did. She loved me coz she loved me granny and I was hers.

But then my granny died.

She died out in our kitchen.

Fell over with the frying pan.

When I found her she wasn't moving.

She was bent funny on the lino floor.

Her face was blue.
And all I could do was scream.

A man called Bob Rooney used to live on Thomas Street.
He used to see me with my granny.
He came to see me after the funeral and said that he'd mind
me.
He gave me a job washing cars.
He showed me how to clean the mop and squeeze just
enough liquid into the handle. He showed me how to power-
hose the wheels and how to polish until every door shined.
He told me I wasn't quick.
He told me I was stupid.
He told me I was too fat and spoilt and couldn't take care of
myself so he had to do it.
He took my purse and said he'd mind it.
He took my Post Office book.
Bob Rooney's son moved into our house and put a caravan in
the back garden.
Bob's Rooney's son locked me in the caravan.
He only let me out in the morning to go to the car wash
which was very far away.
Bob said that no one in Dublin wanted to talk to me.
Bob said that no one in Dublin wanted to know me.
Because they knew I'd killed my granny.
They knew I'd worn her out.
With my fat mouth eating her out of house and home.
And my fat arse taking up half the house.
I told Bob that my granny loved me from the day that I was
born.
So he punched me in my fat mouth.
He punched and punched until two of my teeth came out.
I didn't say anything to Bob Rooney after that.
I didn't say anything to his son.

Not long after I was washing a car.
And who was sitting in the back seat only Gaye from Gaye's
Hairdressers.
She said 'Rita...? Jesus Christ, Rita, is that you?'
I told her it was.

I told her I was sorry that I didn't visit her in the hairdressers.

I told her about the lock and the caravan.

Gaye took out her iPhone and called the police.

Even when Bob's son came out of his hut,

Gaye wouldn't leave.

She picked up the power-hose and started screaming.

People stopped and started to watch.

I could tell that Bob's son wanted to punch her just like he punched me.

But I think he was afraid now.

Afraid that she was too old and that people were watching.

A man came over to ask 'what the fuck was going on'.

Then the police came.

And took me and Gaye away.

The police told me to write my story down, just like this, just like now.

The police told me they would take my story and old Bob Rooney to see a judge.

And Gaye says they'll lock him up in jail.

On account of what he done to me.

On account of what he stole.

And Gaye says that a woman from the council will find me a home in a special place.

Where I will be safe.

And Gaye says that she will come to visit…

MARGARET *has removed her hand from* DOUGLASS*'s face.*

MARGARET. Pardon me sir but I have never seen your like before.

DOUGLASS. Nor I yours.

MARGARET. Will you describe it to me Frederick Douglass.

Will you describe this slavery.

DOUGLASS. It. It is a great evil.

It makes beasts of us all.

MARGARET. All, sir?

DOUGLASS. You stand here and sing Margaret.

You sing to me of subjugation. Of injustice. Of class.

And in America you may well be liberated from your poverty and your race but not on merit alone, not because of your humanity but simply because you are white.

MARGARET. But what is *white*, sir?

DOUGLASS. What is white?

What is white?

White is power, Margaret. White is murder. White is lies. White is money. White is cruelty... great cruelty... boundless cruelty. White is the whip. White is the gun. White is its own ruination, Margaret, because deep down, deep in the bowels of white humanity, they know that slavery is wrong.

MARGARET. It must be, sir.

DOUGLASS. I wonder will you feel the same when you see the power it might grant you?

I wonder will you beat the slave yourself?

MARGARET. Never.

DOUGLASS. Some of your kin do.

MARGARET. My kin?

DOUGLASS. There are Irish slavers, Irish drivers, Margaret.

Irish men and women who crush their black brethren in order to find an American foothold of their own.

MARGARET. Then they have lost their soul Frederick Douglass.

And they have forgotten who they are.

DOUGLASS *now starts to sing 'I Be So Glad When the Sun Goes Down'.*

MARGARET, KABITE *and* RITA *join him.*

I see that you have beautiful songs of your own.

DOUGLASS. I do.

We do.

MARGARET. Wild notes of the cotton field?

DOUGLASS. Indeed. That was my grandmother's song.

My grandmother who raised me. My grandmother who fed me on corn and peaches and dreams.

She fed all of the children on the plantation.

She found us cotton shirts and built a fire that we may be warm.

She gave us laughter and as many living years as she could until...

MARGARET. Until?

DOUGLASS. Until I was old enough to go to work for the master.

When I was taken from her.

When we were all taken from her.

Then we knew what it was to be enslaved.

MARGARET. And what of your mother?

DOUGLASS. I did not know my mother.

MARGARET. You did not know your mother?

DOUGLASS. But briefly, Margaret. My mother was taken herself by the master because the American slave bears children not for herself, not for family but for her master.

The American slave is not human.

The American slave is property.

The American slave is animal.

MARGARET. I cannot, I will not hear of such injustice, sir... in America?!

DOUGLASS. But what I tell you is true.

MARGARET. If it is true, sir!

Where do I go?

Tell me that Mr Frederick Douglass?

Where do I go to find my freedom?

My happiness?

DOUGLASS. Why don't you fight for it here?

MARGARET. With what?

With my two bare hands?

Or would you have me raise a pitchfork like the croppies?

A pitchfork against the English guns?

Two hands against their army?

I tell you, the ground you walk on is steeped in the blood of them that have died fighting for freedom here.

DOUGLASS. But what of your family?

MARGARET. My family?

DOUGLASS. Yes.

MARGARET. Dead too, sir.

DOUGLASS. Dead too?

MARGARET. From hunger.

DOUGLASS. Dear God.

MARGARET. Perhaps he too has forsaken us?

DOUGLASS. Never!

Never!

God is our salvation, Margaret.

MARGARET. Or America?

I thought America was my salvation.

America was my hope.

But now you take that from me Mr Douglass.

With your talk of prejudice, of cruelty and murder.

DOUGLASS. I did not, I do not intend to take anything away from you Margaret.

On the contrary… on the contrary.

I want you and your kin to thrive.

You cannot give up.

We cannot give up.

If I have learnt anything from my years in bondage it is that.

We must trust.

Trust in our message.

Trust in humanity.

And trust that we will find our liberty.

You in America.

MARGARET. And you in Ireland?

DOUGLASS. Perhaps.

Pause.

MARGARET. Then may I be so bold as to caution you, sir.

DOUGLASS. Caution me?

MARGARET. Beware of those fine gentlemen you walked with this morning.

DOUGLASS. They are good people, Margaret.

They believe in the abolition of slavery.

They campaign for it.

They champion the freedom and prosperity of all men.

MARGARET. They do not champion me.

DOUGLASS. All men.

MARGARET. They do not champion mine.

Pause.

But toss us to the sea.

They both look out to the sea.

DOUGLASS. I find this… I find what you tell me about your condition difficult, it is difficult.

MARGARET. Oh aye, it is difficult all right.

DOUGLASS. Because as I said I am only recently arrived…

MARGARET. And you arrive a good man, I can see that.

I can see the truth is in your eyes.

So don't let my masters blind you Mr Douglass.

Don't let my masters take your soul.

Because I fear they only champion your freedom so as to mask their abuse of mine.

Pause.

DOUGLASS. You are a most extraordinary woman, Margaret.

MARGARET. I have to be.

Pause.

Now hadn't I best return to my singing Mr Douglass.

DOUGLASS. I will challenge injustice, Margaret.

I promise you that.

I will challenge injustice wherever I see it no matter what the consequence.

MARGARET. Then Ireland welcomes you, Frederick Douglass.

DOUGLASS. I only hope that America welcomes you.

MARGARET. Why wouldn't it?

DOUGLASS. And all those seeking sanctuary.

Seeking freedom.

Seeking future.

KABITE. Seeking sanctuary.

RITA. Seeking freedom.

KALIEF, *a young black man in a prisoner's uniform, appears*.

KALIEF. Seeking future.

MARGARET. Sure if America turned her back on the likes of me.

Wouldn't America kill the very dream that made her?

KALIEF. I was coming home from a party on Third Avenue. Just walking home when I saw some lights and I knew it was a police car and suddenly the lights were in my eyes and the police officer told me that he had a guy in the car said I robbed him. I said I didn't rob nobody. But the police officer searched me and when he didn't find anything, he said the guy said I tried to rob him. I said I didn't try to rob nobody, I was just walking home. Then another police officer came out of the car and said that I robbed the guy two weeks before. Next thing I know I'm in the car and in the precinct and I'm getting my photograph taken and they taking my fingerprints and I said 'but I didn't do nothing' and they said that I had to plead guilty to go home. But I said I'm not guilty and I said no.

No.

But no nigger gets to say 'no'.

So they posted bail.

But my mama didn't have three thousand dollars.

So I went to jail.

I went to jail for three years without trial.

I want to jail for allegedly robbing a backpack.

I never robbed no backpack.

I left my life in there.

I lost my soul in there.

I hang from my bedroom ceiling.

Like my brother's ghosts still hang from their Southern trees.

I am slave.

KABITE. I am slave.

RITA. I am slave.

DOUGLASS. I want you to succeed, Margaret Keane.

MARGARET. And I want you to succeed Frederick Douglass.

For all of us.

KALIEF/KABITE/RITA. For all of us.

DOUGLASS *starts to sing 'Sweet Caanan's Happy Land'.*

Everyone joins him.

The End.

AN OLD SONG, HALF FORGOTTEN

For Bryan Murray

Author's Note

This play is written to be performed by an actor with
Alzheimer's. The two characters are versions of the one
man, the younger and the older James O'Brien. Older James
O'Brien is currently living with Alzheimer's. Young James is
his memory but also guides him through the play and through
the production, as together they rebuild the man he is through
memories initiated by music.

There are notebooks referred to throughout. I envision they
will contain the script, and be placed around the set to allow
for movement whilst James reads his lines – he is reading his
life as written earlier in the disease – you may also chose to use
an earpiece but I would keep the notebooks and the sense that
James has written his life down as best he can.

A suite of music has been composed by Paul Frost to be
played throughout by a string quartet. The idea being that
James O'Brien is enjoying a performance by the string quartet
currently visiting the day room of his nursing home. From
the outside it looks like a man listening to music but we, the
audience, get to move inside James's head and witness his
memories as sparked by the music and re-enacted by him and
his younger self.

An Old Song, Half Forgotten was first performed on the
Peacock stage at the Abbey Theatre, Dublin, on 14 April 2023.
The cast was as follows:

JAMES   Bryan Murray
YOUNG JAMES   Matthew Malone

Alternate Performer   Barry McGovern
Alternate Performer   Darragh Feehely

Violin   Mia Cooper
Violin   Brigid Leman
Viola   Ed Creedon
Cello   Aoife Burke

Director   Louise Lowe
Set Designer   Conor Jacob
Lighting Designer   Ciaran Bagnall
Sound Designer and
  Additional Composition   Philip Stewart
Costume Designer   Maree Kearns
Composer   Paul Frost
Personal Assistant   Úna Crawford
Creative Producer   Natasha Duffy
Original Music for String Quartet   Paul Frost
Publicity Image   Pat Redmond

Characters

JAMES O'BRIEN, *a dapper man in his seventies*
YOUNG JAMES

A forward slash indicates when the next speaker interrupts/
speaks in unison.

We are in the day room of a nursing home.

There are musicians playing a vigorous piece of classical music.

JAMES O'BRIEN, *a dapper man in his seventies, sits listening appreciatively.*

A YOUNGER MAN *sits by his side, also listening appreciatively.*

The music ends.

JAMES *stands.*

JAMES. Bravo! Bravo!

YOUNG JAMES. Toi! Toi! Toi!

JAMES. Wonderful. Beautiful.

YOUNG JAMES. Mesmeric!

JAMES. Good word, good word, lovely word.

YOUNG JAMES (*to the musicians*). It's the river isn't it?! It's the Liffey. I was born on it you know… bred on it…

JAMES *indicates the very particular notebook from which he reads.*

JAMES. I wrote it, I write it you see, I write it all down.

BOTH. Write it all down.

JAMES. What are the memories I just cannot live without?

BOTH. What are the memories I just cannot live without?

JAMES. That is how I start it.

YOUNG JAMES. Write it. Hold it!

JAMES. Ma's hands.

YOUNG JAMES. My ma's hands.

JAMES. Ma's hands.

Sara's eyes.

Emmet Road.

Danny.

It's all here. Written here.

YOUNG JAMES. Danny Murray. River Liffey. Ma's hands. River Liffey.

JAMES. On that sunny day, that sunny day with Waxer when I take my boy-courage into my hands and jump crazily, crookedly off Island Bridge and into the depths of the River Liffey... when I was what? Seven?

BOTH. Seven.

JAMES. That was the day... my day... the day I find out that I can do anything... ANYTHING. Because I am expressly forbidden from playing on Island Bridge. And I am expressly forbidden from hanging around with Danny Murray and I can tell you, I am expressly forbidden from jumping into the river,

any river,

let alone the River Liffey!

YOUNG JAMES *interjects as his mother – Ma*.

YOUNG JAMES. Jesus, Mary and Joseph!

BOTH. Jesus, Mary and holy saint Joseph...!

YOUNG JAMES (*as Ma*). What do you think you're doing. Dear God! Dear Jesus! you could get diphtheria out of that bloody Liffey... Typhoid! Dysentry! Pneumonia!

JAMES. But it's summer Ma!

YOUNG JAMES (*as Ma*). Don't give me cheek... ya little get, coming in here dripping! Coming in here like a drownded rat and when I told you! Expressly told you never to be going near that river! Who were you with? Sure I don't need to ask! I don't need to ask do I?

JAMES. No she didn't need to ask. Danny Murray.

The musicians play a motif that comes to represent Danny Murray.

That's him!

The musicians play it again.

YOUNG JAMES. That's him! Danny Murray. My best friend, the best friend any boy anywhere could ever hope to call his friend.

JAMES. Danny Murray lives in the small row of cottages on the Alley.

YOUNG JAMES. The Alley, the Alley, the Alley, the Alley…

JAMES. White cottages they are with two families living in each. One on the top floor and one on the bottom floor.

My ma seems to think it is some kind of affliction to live in the 'alley', some great shame or curse that might follow you up-and-out from your breakfast and sit like a threat, a warning on your chest!

YOUNG JAMES (*as Ma*). This fella is bad, this fella is no good… this fella comes from the Alley!

JAMES. But I think it's a great place altogether. Teeming it is.

'The Music of the Alley' comes in.

(*Conducting.*) That's it! That's it! The Alley.

YOUNG JAMES. And always pumping out a smell of potatoes and tobacco and sweat and grease because most of the das work up with the trains in Inchicore or up making beer at Guinness's… and are forever tap-tappin' when they're home, on tin-pans, or old boots or some class of a furnishing. Fixing, threading, heaving, hammering…

Particularly on a sunny day. And it is a sunny day that day
I leap with Danny Murray into the depths of Dublin. The
depths of Dublin's glorious, filthy, rushing river.

The musicians play more of the Liffey music.

The two JAMESES *listen.* YOUNG JAMES *gives old*
JAMES *his notebook and points to the text.*

There are always gangs ringing around the Alley.

JAMES. There are always gangs ringing around the Alley.
Mothers yapping over the half-doors or walking collectively
off over the bridge in their best headscarves to get the bus
into town to do their shopping on Thomas Street, Francis
Street, Meath Street... Camden.

BOTH. And children!

JAMES. Children everywhere.

Children hanging out of the windows.

Children streeling over the cobble.

YOUNG JAMES. Children skipping, jumping, laughing,
screaming. Pelting two hand-balls against the wall of a
cottage or kicking a rag-ball in an effort at soccer.

JAMES. Every cottage in the Alley seems to grow children.
Then chuck them out in a rake of sizes, snot and wild
laughter.

YOUNG JAMES. Then chuck them out in a rake of sizes, snot
and wild laughter.

JAMES. It is a different world to where I live.

A different world to Emmet Road. Yet just around the corner.

YOUNG JAMES. Emmet Road.

A big house. One of the big houses just at the back of
Kilmainham Gaol.

BOTH. It was my grandmother's house.

YOUNG JAMES. And Ma always said that my grandmother was haunted by the volley of shots that rang out when Ireland's patriots were being murdered by the British there in 1916.

JAMES. She did, she always said that.

YOUNG JAMES (*dropping to his knees*). And Ma always said that Granny used to kneel by her bed, hands over her ears, trying to think of lovely things.

JAMES. Lovely things Granny, think of lovely things.

YOUNG JAMES. Because she was only a little girl back then but all she could see in her mind's eye was blood splattering onto the back walls of the gaol and blood running up through our floorboards, seeping into her little-girl world with the terror of it all. And Ma said that she never got over it because if anything every upset Granny she would just close her eyes, drop to the floor and put her hands over her ears. Traumatised, that's what my ma said…

JAMES. Traumatised.

YOUNG JAMES. Lived on her nerves. Lived on her nerves, like Ma.

The musicians play. The two JAMESES *listen.*

JAMES Emmet Road.

Emmet Road.

BOTH. It is an odd kind of a house.

YOUNG JAMES. Our house. Downstairs upstairs.

JAMES. Upstairs downstairs.

YOUNG JAMES. But Ma is fierce proud of it and alway keeps it spotless with a big arrangement of flowers sitting inside the stained glass of the front door.

JAMES Front door.

Front door.

Big Blue Front Door.

BOTH. I can remember.

JAMES. I can remember way back.

I can remember the Alley. I can remember Danny.

But yesterday?! No.

Yesterday is all a fog.

Yesterday is empty.

Yesterday is gone.

YOUNG JAMES. I am your yesterday.

I am my yesterday when we write it all down.

JAMES. Write it. Keep it. Keep / my life.

YOUNG JAMES. My life.

JAMES. Front door.

Lovely things…

YOUNG JAMES. There was just me. Just me living with Ma and Da in the big house.

JAMES. The big house.

YOUNG JAMES. There were others. I know there were brothers but they died. They didn't live beyond infancy. Lost to the mist.

JAMES. Like so many at that time.

YOUNG JAMES. Lost to the few whispers of prayer on an anniversary-I-was-never-told-about but could feel in my bones.

So much unsaid.

So much unsaid in that house. In those days.

JAMES. Who were my brothers?

Brothers in the ground long before I was born.

YOUNG JAMES. Dad works up in the offices. Up in the offices at Guinness so I am not supposed to fraternise with the boys of the Alley but...

JAMES. I always loved Danny Murray.

YOUNG JAMES. I always loved Danny Murray. From the first.

JAMES. Danny Murray is the king, my king.

Danny Murray is top-dog and everyone wants to dance in his shadow.

YOUNG JAMES. Because his strength, his energy, his daring, his laugh, his legs and neck and jaw... Jesus he'd bowl you over.

JAMES. Danny Murray.

YOUNG JAMES. And the height of him as we hit our teens... and the muscle when he went off to work as a cooper with his da, still only fourteen.

JAMES. Fourteen.

YOUNG JAMES. I'll never know why he let me be always, always round him. Always trotting after. I think I might have been eaten alive as a boy in Inchicore if it wasn't for him, his aura, his friendship... that was what kept my skinny, wheezy, timid little arse safe. But he became a man after he left school. He became a man quick...

JAMES. And I lost him.

Somehow I lost him! Lost.

YOUNG JAMES. Lost. Lost.

Lost.

Man after...

JAMES. But then I found the acting. The Acting!

YOUNG JAMES. Oh yes, the Acting.

BOTH. Plough!

> *The two* JAMESES *seem agitated.*

> *Then the music changes.* YOUNG JAMES *responds to the music and begins to set up the stage for a short extract from Seán O'Casey's play* The Plough and the Stars, *where he takes up the role of Young Covey, prompting* JAMES *to respond as Uncle Peter. They recite lines from Act One of the play in which young Covey gently taunts Uncle Peter as they remember their performance.*

YOUNG JAMES (*laughs*). Oh what craic that was!

JAMES. What craic – the acting!

YOUNG JAMES. And I never even knew what it was!

JAMES. Never even knew what it was until we got the television. Never even knew that there was such a thing as acting!

YOUNG JAMES. Never!

JAMES. No, my first sight of the power of it, the magic of it was when Da came home with a television that he rented from a shop up on the Drumcondra Road.

YOUNG JAMES. He planted it in the middle of our front room.

JAMES. He did. He planted it in the middle of our front room.

YOUNG JAMES. And… it was… it was startling!

JAMES. It was like a visit from the zoo!

YOUNG JAMES. The zoo! Because it looked that out of place, that exotic on the old polished sideboard but then oh! Oh!

JAMES. Oh! Oh!

YOUNG JAMES. When we turned it on…

JAMES. Turn it on…!

YOUNG JAMES. And get through the buzz fizz of the black-and-white dotty-floating-scramble for reception, we see what it has to offer!

JAMES. Oh! Oh!

YOUNG JAMES. And we are hooked.

JAMES. And I stand in front of it!

YOUNG JAMES. Face glued to the action and poor Ma pleading – (*As Ma.*) Will you move yourself young Jamesie, you're not the only one watchin' are ya?!

JAMES. *Tolka Row* and *The Twilight Zone…*

Music from The Twilight Zone *filters in.*

YOUNG JAMES. They are my favourites, our favourites because Ma loves it all too… and I can still hear the two of us gasping, clasping across the front-room velvets –

JAMES. Gasping. Clasping.

YOUNG JAMES. – As some unfathomable moment unfolds or some character shatters under the weight of a great emotion… and me always imitating every swoop, every swagger and every movement of every face.

JAMES. The accents, the poise!

YOUNG JAMES. And Ma! (*As Ma.*) Yes yes do it again Jamesie! That's just how that fella Balsam does it, you're a natural!

JAMES. A natural? But a natural what?

YOUNG JAMES (*as Ma*). This country was founded by actors you know, actors and artists and women!

JAMES. Really? They never told us that at school!

YOUNG JAMES. And the da saying 'Did you ever hear such rubbish' but away with her anyway and me by the lapel off up to the Abbey Theatre!

JAMES. The Abbey Theatre!

YOUNG JAMES. 'I'm telling you,' she says to the man at the door, 'this is my son and he's a natural!'

JAMES. Sure how could they resist such a recommendation?!

'This is my son and he's a natural!'

YOUNG JAMES. Frank D.

JAMES. Oh! Oh! Frank D. Magnificent Frank D!

YOUNG JAMES. Frank D, resident director of the Abbey Theatre, takes me in.

JAMES. Magnificent.

YOUNG JAMES. Frank D, resident director of the Abbey Theatre, gives me a chance.

JAMES. He does!

YOUNG JAMES (*as Frank D*). Bollox… that is utter bollox young James… you need to feel it, FEEL it, crucify us with the truth of your performance… crucify us as if we were Jesus up there on the cross!

JAMES. Never met anyone like Frank D.

YOUNG JAMES. And never felt anything like this… this… make-believe.

JAMES. Love it. I just love it!

YOUNG JAMES. Make-believe that I am an actor. Make-believe that I am a man. Make-believe that I am strong, sure of myself… dashing… dandy… dapper… thoughtful… worthy… worthwhile…

JAMES. In this new world. This dazzling new world of light and truth and words and emotion. Such emotion. High emotion! Huge emotion! Unstopped. Unchartered. And all said, everything said. Not like life on Emmet Road.

Am I on Emmet Road?

I'm not. I am not. Where am I?

YOUNG JAMES. In the wings! In the wings of the Abbey
Theatre on that first night of that first play… *The Hostage*.

JAMES. Oh yes. Oh yes!

YOUNG JAMES (*as Frank D*). Crucify!

JAMES. I remember. I do remember. I remember the sound of
it, the heat of it… that first play.

YOUNG JAMES. Oh! Oh!

JAMES. And the heat of the audience… the feel of the
audience… out there… out there in the darkness… out there
stealing our breath, my breath… living on it, my breath…
feeding on it, my breath… my speech… my words. And
when I kissed, kissed a girl, my girl in that play then I could
feel hearts stop out there in the darkness. Hearts quiver out
there in the darkness. Hearts turn. Hearts hate. Hearts envy.

And I remember Frank D after the curtain went down.

I remember Frank D whisper:

YOUNG JAMES (*as Frank D*). Well done young James, well
done young man… when you kissed that girl… you kissed
the world.

JAMES. The world! The world! Imagine! This life. This theatre.
This *acting* that Frank D gave me. That Ma gave me. Well, it
opened up everything, everyone, everyone that is dear to me.

It opened up the world.

YOUNG JAMES. London!

JAMES. London!

'London Calling' by The Clash comes crashing in. YOUNG
JAMES *gets all punky, miming singing it and interacting
with older* JAMES, *who enjoys it all immensely. Both join in
for some of the lyrics.*

YOUNG JAMES. Apollo Theatre, Lyric Theatre, Piccadilly
    Theatre.

JAMES. Her Majesty's, St James's, Old Vic. I played them all.

YOUNG JAMES. I played them all.

JAMES. Bigger than the Abbey! Better than the Abbey!

    But not the Abbey. Not Dublin. Not home.

    I'm not home. I am not home. Where am I?

YOUNG JAMES. Ma came, didn't she? Ma came.

    (*As Ma.*) My son! my son! My son is in the West End!

JAMES. Six years, after six years in the Abbey. London.

YOUNG JAMES. West End.

JAMES. And I am a young man now. I am a real man now.

YOUNG JAMES. Heading off.

    Vrooom vroom!

JAMES. Setting off. Vroom vroom! To a new life.

    So I go to see Danny. Go to see all the gang from the Alley to
    say goodbye.

YOUNG JAMES. Lovely things.

    Why not just think of lovely things?

JAMES. Because that's not honest.

    That's not all of it, is it? All of my life.

YOUNG JAMES. All of my life.

JAMES. I go to see Danny Murray. Down at the Patriot Inn.
    And he is drinking with the men from Guinness's. Drinking
    with his father on a Friday night. And they welcome me in.
    And we have a right night of it. I remember.

    The pub was packed. I remember.

And we are all elbow to elbow in the heave of it... thigh to thigh in the din of it... and we are singing... and they wish me luck, feed me pints... 'the actor!', 'their actor!' Till I am sick as a dog and have to stumble outside. Stumble home... with the help of Danny. And we both laughing, and we both stumbling...

YOUNG JAMES. I love you.

JAMES. I love you, Danny Murray.

YOUNG JAMES. And I miss you in my life.

JAMES. I miss you since you went to Guinness's. I miss you Danny.

And then I kiss him. Kiss him gently on the cheek. Kiss him gently on the lips and he does, he does something startling.

YOUNG JAMES. Danny Murray kisses back.

JAMES. And I get such a surprise, such a shock that I stop. And Jesus, his face! Danny's face... Danny's face. Before he punches out, before he pounds, pounding pounding me with his fist, my head... with his fist, my chest...with his fist... my eyes, my mouth. And his anger. Such deadly deadly anger...

YOUNG JAMES (*as Danny*). That never fucking happened! Right James...?

You better tell me that that never fucking happened or I'll have to kill you right here in the Alley.

JAMES. Right! Right! It never happened.

Never happened, Danny.

YOUNG JAMES (*as Danny*). Now fuck off to London, you little queer, I hope I never see you again.

JAMES. I hope I never see you again!

And we didn't.

I didn't.

Not for years. Poor Danny. Poor Danny Murray. What happened? What happened Danny Murray?

The musicians begin to play a piece of music.

The two JAMESES *stop to listen.*

YOUNG JAMES. Apollo Theatre, Lyric Theatre, Picadilly Theatre.

JAMES. Her Majesty's, St James's, Old Vic… I played them all!

YOUNG JAMES. I played them all.

Found Sara.

JAMES. Sara. My Sara. And I simply cannot forget her.

YOUNG JAMES. What are the memories I just cannot live without?

JAMES. Sara. My Sara.

If I forget her I am lost. If I forget her then I no longer want to be. I simply no longer want to be.

YOUNG JAMES. I will write her down. Write it all down…

JAMES. I'm tired of this. I think I am tired of this. So bloody tired of it all…

YOUNG JAMES. Searching. Searching. Always searching.

JAMES. Searching. Searching. Always searching.

The rest of this speach is in unision but jagged/speaking over each other.

BOTH. Trying to find! Trying to root… deep down… deep down through the stony grey soil of memory. Digging… always digging… until my head hurts… until my head pains… and turning up what? Down there in the muck of me… just muddy pictures… or confused moments… or empty faces.

Empty faces.

JAMES. I cannot lose Sara...

YOUNG JAMES. I am doing... I am doing... I am doing??

JAMES. *The Importance of Being Earnest.*

YOUNG JAMES. That's it! That's it!

JAMES. Who cares? I can't change this. Can't change looking out at a world that no longer makes sense.

Can't change trying to trust. Trying to trust my mind. My mind!

YOUNG JAMES. Trying to trust.

JAMES. Can't change the anger.

Raging / anger.

YOUNG JAMES. / Anger at the inconvenience of others. Other people walking in my way. Other people walking through my home. Other people walking through my life and faces... faces pale, faces shocked, faces blurring, twisting, melting... becoming unfamiliar... like my world...

JAMES. Like the streets that I have traversed for decades gradually moving, gradually shifting, turning different corners onto different streets and I am lost.

Sara?

Where is Sara? I need her with me.

I try to hold! I try to pretend. I look at the face by my side, the face of my wife, my daughter, my friend and I wonder who they are, why they are / so slow...

YOUNG JAMES. So slow so slow to see that I am here, that I am hungry, that I am tired... and then I just cannot find the word to tell them... or I cannot find the key –

JAMES. The stupid key –

YOUNG JAMES. The key to the car, the key to the shed, the key to the door, the key to my life because my life... my inner life... my inside life of words and pictures and smells

and faces and passions and discoveries and laughter and taste
and glorious-story fades, fogs, freezes, melts and I can't find
it, I can't find them, I can't find me.

JAMES. I can't find me.

Me. Me. Me. Me. Me. Me. Me. Me. Me. Me. Me. Me. Me.

YOUNG JAMES. Sara.

Tweed skirt. Satin blouse.

JAMES. I'm too tired.

YOUNG JAMES. Tweed skirt. Satin blouse. Suede shoes.

JAMES. I'm not interested.

YOUNG JAMES. Eyes lifting as I take my seat.

Eyes lifting behind fashionable reading glasses.

Tweed skirt. Satin blouse.

JAMES. It was a two-piece actually.

YOUNG JAMES. It was a two-piece actually.

JAMES. Very de rigueur. Very Mary Quant. And short!...
Daringly short... in an emerald green!

YOUNG JAMES. Sara's knees...

JAMES. Sara's knees...

YOUNG JAMES. Squeezed tight in that pencil of emerald
green.

JAMES. Emerald green.

And that would have been no accident you know! Not with
Sara. No, no. So learned. So wise. So wide-ranging in her
thinking, her approach... to theatre, to life! Way ahead of
me... always. Yes, that emerald green would have been
carefully chosen for that first morning, that first reading of an
Irish play in a troubled time by a troubled man.

YOUNG JAMES. She played Gwendolen.

JAMES. Gwendolen! Gwendolen. God what a gas…! What a laugh…! Always… always with Wilde… wild laughter to hide all our anguish.

And it was a time of anguish, great anguish.

YOUNG JAMES. For Ireland.

JAMES. For Ireland. For Irish in London.

There is a crashing sound and YOUNG JAMES *now throws himself to his knees.*

YOUNG JAMES. Bombs!

JAMES. Bombs.

YOUNG JAMES. Bombs for Ireland.

JAMES. Bombs for Ireland.

Bombs in Birmingham. Bombs in Manchester. Bombs in the city.

Dreadful. Dreadful it was. A dreadful time to be Irish.

YOUNG JAMES. Yet there she sat, Miss Sara Walsh in her emerald green.

JAMES. Miss Sara Walsh.

Miss Gwendolen Fairfax.

YOUNG JAMES. Miss Gwendolen Fairfax. Oh! Oh!

YOUNG JAMES *excitedly sets up the stage for them both to play a scene from* The Importance of Being Earnest *by Oscar Wilde. He gives* JAMES *a cue to start the scene – setting him up with the script to read, etc.*

JAMES (*as Jack*). Ever since I met you I have admired you more than any girl… I have ever met since I met you.

I like that. I really like that.

YOUNG JAMES. So say it again.

JAMES (*as Jack*). Ever since I met you I have admired you more than any girl… I have ever met since I met you.

YOUNG JAMES (*as Gwendolen*). Yes I am quite well aware of the fact. And I often wish that in public, at any rate, you had been more demonstrative. For me you have always had an irresistible fascination. Even before I met you I was far from indifferent to you.

JAMES (*as Jack*). Really!

YOUNG JAMES (*as Gwendolen*). We live as I hope you know Mr Worthing in a world of ideals. The fact is often mentioned in the more expensive monthly magazines, and has reached the provincial pulpits I am told; and my ideal has always been to love someone by the name of Ernest. There is something in that name that inspires absolute confidence. The moment Algernon first mentioned that he had a friend called Ernest I knew I was destined to love you.

JAMES. You really love me Gwendolen?

YOUNG JAMES. Passionately!

JAMES. Darling! You don't know how happy you've made me!

YOUNG JAMES. My own Ernest!

JAMES. But you don't really mean to say that you couldn't love me if my name wasn't Ernest?

YOUNG JAMES. But your name is Ernest?

JAMES. Yes, I know it is. But supposing it was something else? Do you mean to say you couldn't love me then? Because personally, darling, to speak quite candidly, I don't care much about the name of Ernest... I don't think the name suits me at all!

YOUNG JAMES. It suits you perfectly. It is a divine name. It has a music of its own. It produces vibrations.

Vibrations indeed!

JAMES. Vibrations indeed!

The song 'She Loves You' by The Beatles blasts in. YOUNG JAMES *starts singing it too. He invites older* JAMES *to dance. The two of them dance happily to the song. The two of them then sit down.*

YOUNG JAMES. London. Sara. London.

JAMES. London. Sara. London

Trotting out into Leicester Square. Soho. Covent Garden. Day trips out to Hampton Court… that's where Sara hails from.

YOUNG JAMES. Beautiful.

JAMES. So beautiful out there on the river. So different to Dublin, to Emmet Road.

YOUNG JAMES. Wealthy, rooted, assured.

JAMES. And the city. Oh wow, the city…

YOUNG JAMES *dances through this to the light impression of 'She Loves You'.*

The lights… the dances… the bars… the curries!

I mean who in Inchicore had ever had a curry?!

And actors, and directors, and writers, and dancers but not like home, not like the Abbey… they are confident… so confident and so flash with their fancy accents and fancy threads and lots to say, oodles to say about…

YOUNG JAMES. Theatre, politics, life, arrrrrt!

JAMES. Yet they welcome me in. Welcome me in because of Sara.

It is Sara who gives me my life in London.

Sara who gives me everything now.

Sara who is my greatest happiness.

YOUNG JAMES (*as Ma*). Ooh is that a fact!?

JAMES. Ma!

YOUNG JAMES. Ma.

JAMES. I think I love her, Ma.

YOUNG JAMES (*as Ma*). You think you love her?

JAMES. Yes.

YOUNG JAMES (*as Ma*). Well don't be hanging round then son.

Girls like Sara Walsh don't grow on trees!

JAMES. Ma!

Ma, Ma, Ma, Ma, Ma!

YOUNG JAMES. Ma loves London!

JAMES. Ma loves coming to London.

Ma loves coming to London in her big velvet hat.

YOUNG JAMES. Sitting in the front row of the theatre blocking out half the stage.

JAMES. She almost causes a riot!

YOUNG JAMES (*as Ma*). That's my son! My son! James O'Brien. James O'Brien! Do you see him? Do you see?

He's the one playing Ernest, isn't he marvellous! Isn't he great...! Sure the others might as well not be there... the others might as well pack up and go home... because my James, my Jamesie steals the show. See the way he moves! See the way he owns that stage! He trained at the Abbey Theatre you know... that's the Abbey Theatre, Dublin... and he has more lines than any of them! Oh and isn't he a heartbreaker in that suit?! He's filled out great I have to say... eating all the muck you serve up over here... I tell you I wouldn't touch most of the food in that Soho but he swears by it...

JAMES. Laden with sausages. Always.

Laden with papers. Always.

And full of news.

YOUNG JAMES (*as Ma*). Phylis Murphy is suffering fierce
   with the bladder. Got an operation up in James's but sure it
   makes no difference. Drownded she is half the time. God
   love her, but sure what chance do you have after twelve
   children?

   And Mr McIntyre at number twelve died four days ago, I just
   made the funeral yesterday before taking the boat. His poor
   wife is stricken and the two sons drinking for Ireland... have
   they no respect! And Mrs Murray round the Alley still has
   cancer. She says to say hello.

JAMES. Mrs Murray. Mrs Murray. Danny's ma?

YOUNG JAMES (*as Ma*). And your father sends his love. He
   doesn't like the plays much, as you know, and we were afraid
   his chest might play up in the spray of the journey. I'll bring
   him back some peppermints. He liked that tin of peppermints
   we got him in that posh shop last time.

   Now have you asked that lovely girl to marry you yet?!

JAMES. Ah!

YOUNG JAMES (*as Ma*). I won't rest lest I know you've got
   someone good to look after you over here Jamesie. And she
   has a good heart, I can see it. And she loves you, I can see
   that too. And she's Catholic, thank God! I was only terrified
   you'd get mixed up with a Protestant over here. She's perfect.

   Well I know she's English but you can't have everything.

   So don't be hanging around, son.

   Girls like Sara Walsh don't grow on trees!

JAMES. Girls like Sara Walsh don't grow on trees.

   Ma's last gift.

YOUNG JAMES (*as Ma*). Marry her now! Marry Sara, James.

JAMES. Ma's last gift to me.

YOUNG JAMES. Because she dies.

   Ma dies. Not long after.

JAMES. And Da sits on his own on Emmet Road.

In front of the telly. Which is quiet now.

Quiet.

Like all the ghosts of the house.

'London Music' rises and plays for a minute or two.

YOUNG JAMES. London. Sara. London.

JAMES. Mrs Murray. Ma. Danny.

He comes to London. Danny.

YOUNG JAMES. He comes to London when?

A few years. A few years after Ma is gone.

JAMES. And I'm a celebrity now.

I am a household name!

YOUNG JAMES. I am on the inside of the telly.

JAMES. I am a detective on *The Bill*.

I am a Dalek out to get *Doctor Who*.

YOUNG JAMES. I am Billy big-balls doing all the best plays, doing all the best parts and all the best telly.

And I think I'm in Kilburn. Yes, it is Kilburn. Opening night at the Tricycle, some Irish play, some Irish heart and Sara and I...

JAMES. Sara and I are leaving the theatre.

Sara and I are walking to our car.

...with guests, two guests.

BBC producers. Flash.

And there he is...

YOUNG JAMES. There he is. Danny Murray.

Torn. Drunk. Small.

Danny?! How?

JAMES. James. He says. James.

YOUNG JAMES (*as Danny*). Is that you Jamesie?

JAMES. But I remember the kiss.

And I remember his fist.

So I don't look.

And I don't answer.

YOUNG JAMES. So I don't look.

And I don't answer.

The music stops. They both look at the musicians. They are taking a break, possibly leaving the stage.

Time for tea.

JAMES. Time for tea.

They sit and await their tea.

JAMES. I am in London now… I am in London now aren't I?

YOUNG JAMES. London.

JAMES. Is that where I live?

I wonder if there is apple tart with tea.

YOUNG JAMES. I love my apple tart.

JAMES. Sara makes it.

Ma used to make it but Ma was no cook.

YOUNG JAMES. No.

JAMES. Burnt to a crisp every time.

YOUNG JAMES. Lives on her nerves.

JAMES. Everything boiled or baked out of existence for fear of germs.

YOUNG JAMES. And Da's dentures.

JAMES. I am in London now aren't I?

YOUNG JAMES. I am in London.

JAMES. Could be anywhere.

YOUNG JAMES. Could be anywhere.

JAMES. Because nothing looks the same... nothing fits... nothing feels like home.

YOUNG JAMES. Oakwood Residential...

JAMES. That's what it says on the plaque.

Oakwood. And not an oak in sight.

I miss home. I miss the green of the Phoenix Park. The din of the street. The whoosh of the river and the feel of it... underground... flowing... flowing... flowing on.

This world is grey. Very grey.

Everything is stone. Even in the garden.

Pebble stone and gravel stone and patio and...

Not an oak in sight.

YOUNG JAMES. I miss the music.

JAMES. The music was nice.

A PORTER *hands* JAMES *his tea and apple tart.*

Ah! Wonderful. Wonderful. Thank you so much!

Apple tart.

And with a sprinkle of sugar on the crust.

Perfect.

YOUNG JAMES. A sprinkle, just a sprinkle like Sara does it.

JAMES. Sara's the best. The best at apple tart.

Best at everything.

YOUNG JAMES. I landed on my feet.

JAMES. Landed on my feet with Sara.

Where is Sara? Will she come? Or is she busy? Busy in the kitchen. Busy with her classes. Busy with Sorcha running their workshops... Mindfulness, yoga...

YOUNG JAMES. Qigong!

JAMES. And she makes a living at it?

You can make a living at it! – Qigong. I mean who knew?

YOUNG JAMES. Esther Road.

JAMES. Sounds familiar.

YOUNG JAMES. Esther Road.

JAMES. Of course. Of course. Our house. Our house on Esther Road. Esther Road is home. Esther Road, London. And Sara loves it... Sara loves our house... Victorian tiles in the hall. Cushions. Crack in the fireplace. My old green comfy chair...

YOUNG JAMES. Those Victorian tiles were a bitch...

JAMES. A bitch to uncover!!

Years of lino, you see.

YOUNG JAMES. Steaming off all the glue...

JAMES. And Sara in those ridiculous goggles!

YOUNG JAMES. But still beautiful.

JAMES. Oh God she is beautiful.

Pause.

YOUNG JAMES. Nearly lost her. Nearly lost Sara too.

JAMES. Nearly lost her! My God, I nearly lost Sara.

Cannot forget her. Cannot let that face fade, Sara's face fade.

YOUNG JAMES. Write it. Write her.

JAMES. Nearly lost her once.

Cannot lose her again. Then I am not me. Not me.

YOUNG JAMES. I thought it was the babies.

JAMES. Stupid. Stupid me. I thought it was the babies.

YOUNG JAMES. Losing those two babies…early… just clots of blood… outbursts… didn't even go to the hospital and I said 'sure we can try again, go again… it's natural, isn't it? It happens to women' but to Sara… well. She planted two flowerbeds in the garden on Esther Road. Named them. Filled them with roses. And then… nothing. Not for years. No pregnancy.

I always thought it was the babies made her sad.

JAMES. But it was me.

It was me.

YOUNG JAMES. Billy big-balls strutting through London in his successful life.

(*As Sara*.) I don't know who you are any more.

JAMES. I don't know who you are any more, James.

Christ! And she was leaving.

Sara leaving!

YOUNG JAMES. Quite determined. Out the door. Solicitor's letter.

(*As Sara*.) It's not enough for me. This is not enough for me. Theatre is not enough.

JAMES. But I thought we were happy!

YOUNG JAMES (*as Sara*). No, you are happy.

JAMES. Christ. What to do?! What to do?!

I cannot lose you, Sara... I can't... give me time.

YOUNG JAMES. Vroom vroom.

JAMES. Vroom vroom.

YOUNG JAMES *sets up the chairs so that he can sit in front, and he sits* JAMES *on the back like a motorbike.*

YOUNG JAMES. And we're off!

JAMES. That summer.

YOUNG JAMES. That summer. What a summer. Our summer. Sara's summer. We take to the road and we are reborn.

JAMES. Take to the road in Dublin.

Take to the road over mountains.

Take to the road going west.

YOUNG JAMES. Silver lakes. Purple mountains. Low singing patchwork walls. Wind and rain. Wind and rain over ancient green.

I can hear her laughter. Sara's laughter. And feel her arms tight around me.

JAMES. Dip in the nip!

YOUNG JAMES. Dip in the nip!

JAMES. Let's take a dip in the nip in these Connemara waters.

YOUNG JAMES. Lough Inagh. Oh! Oh!

JAMES. Lough Inagh!

YOUNG JAMES. In the shadow of the convent. In the garden of the nuns.

Two daring lovers, me and Sara, no longer young but loving.

JAMES. Two sun-kissed bodies kissing.

YOUNG JAMES. White flesh and pink love and silver rippling water. Not lost. Not lost. We are not lost.

JAMES. Oh! Oh! Back in the water. Back in the water.

Like Waxer!

YOUNG JAMES. Waxer?! Waxer Doolin?!

Not in Connemara.

JAMES. No not in Connemara.

Waxer's Dublin. All Dublin.

YOUNG JAMES *now gets off the motorbike and takes up position to become an old neighbour, Waxer Doolin, marching out of his house and down to the river. Once he starts the walk,* JAMES *speaks.*

Waxer Doolin lives in the last house on the Alley.

Waxer Doolin has no one, no family.

Waxer Doolin hibernates for the winter but then, as sure as the return of the swallow, Waxer will emerge in his tattered long johns to take his spring jump off the bridge and into the Liffey.

YOUNG JAMES. Go Waxer! Go Waxer! Swim Waxer! Swim Waxer!

JAMES. It is Waxer Doolin calls in our summer. And it is Waxer Doolin shows us how to swim.

YOUNG JAMES (*as Waxer*). Keep your heads up, your arses down and kick! Kick for Ireland! Kick for the sons of 1916. Kick like bejaysus!

Did you know that man was once amphibian? He was! He just lost his fins. To be in the water is a natural state, boys. As natural as it is to be eating a bag of chips. So breathe, breathe hard, suck the air right down to your ankles and jump to fuck… Jump in and kick. You'll be grand.

JAMES. You'll be grand!

YOUNG JAMES. And we jump! And Danny is the strongest. Danny is a fish. Danny hurls through the water with his boy-legs already iron. Danny's long hair is wet, flat black against his smile. Danny sees I'm frozen. Danny sees I'm struggling. Danny pulls me up by the scruff of the neck, up, up, up and into the clear screaming air of Dublin.

JAMES. Danny holds me up like a trophy.

Danny wraps me up in his jumper and deposits me on the step by the blue front door. When I was what?

BOTH. Seven.

JAMES. So how come they pull the body of Danny Murray out of the river one spring morning? One spring morning years after? How?

YOUNG JAMES (*as Danny*). Now fuck off to London, you little queer, I hope I never see you again.

JAMES. I'm sorry I never turned.

I'm sorry I never answered.

Because I know you wouldn't drown, Danny.

Unless you wanted to.

YOUNG JAMES. ...wouldn't drown, Danny.

Unless you wanted to.

The string quartet return from their break to take their seats.

The two JAMESES *note this and take their seats to listen.*

The music starts. They listen.

JAMES. Ah, that's beautiful.

YOUNG JAMES (*quietly*). Bravo. Bravo.

Sounds like Sara, doesn't it? Sounds like Sorcha.

JAMES. Sometimes I think they are one and the same.

YOUNG JAMES. We brought Sorcha back from Ireland that summer.

Sorcha back from Lough Inagh.

Secreted away in the womb of us.

Ireland's daughter.

Ireland's gift.

JAMES. Life complete.

YOUNG JAMES. Life complete.

JAMES. Is it Sorcha who comes?

I think it is?

YOUNG JAMES. Sorcha.

JAMES. With books.

With apple tart.

YOUNG JAMES (*as Sorcha*). Out to lunch. Out to lunch today, Daddy.

JAMES. That's right. In her little car. Oh, and I just want to stroke her face as she is driving, as she is talking, stroke her cheek like when she was little...

YOUNG JAMES. But she is concentrating.

JAMES. Of course she is, she is watching the road and she is telling me all about her play because... because she is an actor, she is a writer!

YOUNG JAMES. Yes. Yes.

JAMES. Followed her old man into the theatre!

YOUNG JAMES. Yes.

JAMES. Got the writing from her mother.

Bright, so bright... like her mother.

Will she come today I wonder?

YOUNG JAMES. Might do.

Might do.

JAMES. Might come today.

Joy. Pure joy. From the day she was born, Sorcha.

YOUNG JAMES. Gurgles.

JAMES. Gurgles.

YOUNG JAMES. Giggles.

JAMES. Giggles.

YOUNG JAMES. Baby sounds. All those little baby sounds
and babygros… cotton or fleece with the button-under and
Sara sleeping soundly and my turning to the big blue eyes…
big blue baby eyes looking out from between the bars of the
crib… and up for a feed. Up for a feed in the dead of night,
just us, just the two of us, me and baby, me and Sorcha in the
deep dark still of the world.

I'll write it. Keep writing it.

JAMES. To hold it.

YOUNG JAMES. Her head and Sara's head intertwined… same
curls, same intellect, same beauty… bending over a book.

And laughter at the dinner table.

Laughter in the garden.

Then off to school. Off to ballet. Off to drama. Off to uni. Off
out into life… glorious life, precious life.

JAMES. Vrooooom vrooooom.

YOUNG JAMES *laughs*.

YOUNG JAMES. Vroooom vroooom.

Pause as they listen to another swirl of music.

Tweed skirt. Satin blouse. Suede shoes.

Eyes lifting as I take my seat.

Eyes lifting behind fashionable reading glasses.

Tweed skirt. Satin blouse.

JAMES. It was a two-piece actually.

YOUNG JAMES. It was a two-piece actually.

JAMES. Very de rigueur. Very Mary Quant. And short…!
Daringly short… in an emerald green!

YOUNG JAMES. Sara's knees…

JAMES. Sara's knees…

YOUNG JAMES. Squeezed tight in that pencil of emerald
green.

JAMES. Emerald green.

And that would have been no accident you know! Not with
Sara. No, no. So learned. So wise. So wide-ranging in her
thinking, her approach… to theatre, to life! Way ahead of
me… always. Yes, that emerald green would have been
carefully chosen for that first morning, that first reading of an
Irish play in a troubled time by a troubled man.

YOUNG JAMES. She played Gwendolen.

JAMES. Gwendolen! Gwendolen. God what a gas…! What a
laugh…! Always… always with Wilde… wild laughter to
hide all our anguish.

And it was a time of anguish, great anguish.

YOUNG JAMES. For Ireland.

JAMES. For Ireland. For Irish in London.

YOUNG JAMES. Bombs!

JAMES. Bombs.

YOUNG JAMES. Bombs for Ireland.

JAMES. Bombs for Ireland.

Bombs in Birmingham. Bombs in Manchester. Bombs in the city.

Dreadful. Dreadful it was. A dreadful time to be Irish.

YOUNG JAMES. Yet there she sat, Miss Sara Walsh in her emerald green.

JAMES. Miss Sara Walsh.

Miss Gwendolen Fairfax.

YOUNG JAMES. Miss Gwendolen Fairfax. Oh! Oh!

(*As if realising for the first time*.) Sara's dead.

Sara's dead.

JAMES. Yes, yes.

Sara's dead.

YOUNG JAMES. It is Sorcha who comes. Sorcha who cares for me isn't it? Sorcha.

Sara's not out there in the world.

JAMES. Sara's not out there in the world but I cannot forget her.

I don't forget her. Sara is in here. (*Pointing to his heart*.)

Sara is my life. My life with Sara is me.

YOUNG JAMES. Me, me, me, me, me, me, me, me, me.

JAMES. I have her here.

YOUNG JAMES. I have her here.

YOUNG JAMES *lifts the book up to show the musicians*.

I have Sara here so I can see her any morning.

Conjur every morning.

JAMES. Like that first morning.

YOUNG JAMES. Still with me. They are all still with me.

Ma, Da, Danny, Frank, Sara... even if the voices fade, even when the features fade –

JAMES. Even when memory fails.

Even when the mind fails.

The world I love, the ones I love continue to roam, continue to live, continue to sing, deep down in the artery.

YOUNG JAMES. Deep down in the artery.

JAMES. In the arteries of me.

Me, me, me, me, me, me, me, me, me, me, me, me, me, me, me...

YOUNG JAMES. Deep down.

BOTH. Me.

JAMES. Me.

The music swells up, plays, and then swirls back into the piece played at the beginning, with JAMES *and* YOUNG JAMES *taking up the exact position as at the start of the play. They are listening appeciatively.*

The music ends.

The two men stand up and applaud.

The musicians take a bow for the residents.

The two men clap and clap and clap.

The lights fade.

The End.

www.nickhernbooks.co.uk

facebook.com/nickhernbooks

twitter.com/nickhernbooks